MEDITATION

and the

MIND of MAN

BASED ON THE EDGAR CAYCE READINGS

by Herbert B. Puryear, Ph.D.
and
Mark A. Thurston, Ph.D.

Revised, Enlarged Edition

A.R.E. PRESS • VIRGINIA BEACH • VIRGINIA

. . .how much greater is a day in the house of the Lord—or a moment in His presence—than a thousand years in carnal forces? 262-57

CONTENTS

PREFACE

One of the most promising developments of the past ten years has been the blossoming of a widespread interest in meditation. The life and work of Edgar Cayce have no doubt made a significant contribution to this awakening. More than forty years ago he was encouraging people in the practice of an approach to meditation which he intimated was based on the purpose and manner in which Jesus Himself taught meditation.

For this reason we are pleased to be able to offer this book based upon the readings given on this vast and vitally important subject. The present study is from a psychological point of view; it is hoped that books from other perspectives will be drawn from this invaluable information given by Edgar Cayce.

This book had its origins in its present form in 1972 when I developed a three-part presentation entitled, *Meditation and the Mind of Man.* Tapes of this course were made and the transcriptions were considered for publication; but alas, the spoken word falls far short of the more stringent requirements needed in print.

At that time, Mark Thurston offered to reorganize and rewrite the text. He added extensive documentation from the readings and other sources and he also added the chapter on ideals.

Later, with the development of the A.R.E. research project on meditation, Mark Thurston and I worked in close collaboration again on a step-by-step manual on how to meditate—now found in Chapter 7. Mark Thurston was responsible for writing this manual in its present highly detailed and beautifully organized format.

Following the first rewrite, several students of meditation read the manuscript and made helpful suggestions which were incorporated in our final rewriting. This second edition now contains a re-editing of the whole text and expansion of the section on affirmations and physiology.

The book is not intended to be a definitive text on meditation. Certain important principles are stressed and others only alluded to or sometimes not covered at all. The very frequent references to Lama Govinda's *Foundations of Tibetan Mysticism* and to the ancient Taoist text on meditation entitled *The Secret of the Golden Flower* are stressed to give the reader a perspective of the universal quality of the information which came through the Christ-oriented superconscious of Edgar Cayce.

When we find the Bible, Edgar Cayce, Tibetan Buddhism and ancient Taoism in agreement on so many principles, we may sense a discovery of universal laws; for example, all of these sources emphasize the importance of the mind and none of them promises an easy way. It is hoped that the meditator will find not only these comparative quotations but the books themselves to be helpful.

In addition to these two texts, we especially recommend the two major series of Edgar Cayce readings which are published in the A.R.E. Library Series, *Meditation, Part I* (which is the 281 series), *Meditation, Part II,* and the *Study Group Readings* (which is the 262 series). These volumes give a very complete and extremely helpful coverage of the Edgar Cayce information on meditation. The student will also want to read *Venture Inward* by Hugh Lynn Cayce, and *Meditation— Gateway to Light* by Elsie Sechrist.

Herbert Bruce Puryear, Ph.D.

Chapter One

FUNDAMENTAL CONCEPTS OF
THE NATURE OF MAN

The central teaching of the Edgar Cayce readings is best understood by seeing the oneness in this triune formula: *the Spirit is the life, Mind is the builder, the Physical is the result.* This formula is the basis for the understanding of the nature of man which is given in the readings; and oneness in the triune is the key to our understanding of the way in which the readings approach the subject of meditation. Let us examine this formula briefly.

The Spirit is the life. All life, indeed all that exists, is a manifestation of the one creative energy, which is God. All force is one force. There is, in the universe, only one energy, but it manifests through many patterns and forms. The energy of electricity and the energy we use to get angry are the same energy. The energy of an atomic explosion and the energy of sexual expression are simply different manifestations of this one energy. Since there are different energy or motivational centers in our bodies, it is difficult to rise above the illusion that we have a certain amount of sexual energy, a certain amount of work energy, and a certain amount of anger energy, and that these energies can be expressed only in those particular forms. Such an illusion leads to a form of idolatry, a belief in many gods: a god of love, a god of work, a god of war, etc. Whenever we believe that we cannot transform energy which might be expressed negatively into a more creative or loving expression, we are believing in the concept of many gods. In contrast to this, the readings stress the understanding that "The Lord thy God is One."

O, that all men would know, "Know, O ye children of men, the Lord thy God is *One!*" Each Spirit, each manifestation of *Life* is *One,* and a manifestation either in this, that or the other sphere, or scope, or space of development towards the knowledge, the understanding, the conception of that *One—Him—I AM—God—* Jehovah—Yah Weh—*all One!*   262-32

For all force, all power that is manifested in thyself, is of the *One* source.   1494-1

1

The first lesson for *six months* should be ONE—One—One— *One;* Oneness of God, oneness of man's relation, oneness of force, oneness of time, oneness of purpose, *oneness* in every effort—oneness—oneness! 900-429

Mind is the builder. It is with the mind that this one energy is given form. Mind acts to give shape and pattern to the life force. The shapes and forms, created by the mind, energized by the one force, manifest as our physical world.

Q-12. Let the light represent the Spiritual, the film the physical faculties of the senses (mind), and the moving picture on the screen this physical life—talking, feeling, tasting, thinking, emotion, etc., and one has a good comparison. Changing pictures, but One Fixed Light. A-12. Correct. 900-156

For, that we find in the spirit taketh form in the mind. Mind becomes the builder. 3359-1

Mind is of central importance in man's activities. One of the most challenging concepts in the readings is that *Mind is the Way;* therefore, understanding Mind is deeply significant for our understanding of meditation. Meditation may even be defined as the practice of a very special and efficacious mode of the principle that Mind is the Builder. *The Physical is the result.* Our bodies, our behavior patterns, and the material world which we experience about us are the results, the effects, of that which has been built by the mind. We must come to accept responsibility for the fact that we are co-creators with God. Through meditation we are creating that which we will become both temporally and eternally. It behooves us to consider fully what it is that we want to become, and to understand the relationship between the continual working of the mind and the subsequent physical manifestation of those same thoughts.

. . . thoughts create those conditions that become as actualities in material forces . . . Hence the lessons, as has oft been given, as to how one in one's mental being may create those conditions that bring about just such physical results. 136-82

The mental body is the *builder,* and the *effects* of that as guided by the forces of life through the spiritual forces, in the atomic forces of system, are manifested in the material or physical body. 197-1

2

If oneness is the central principle in the readings, why do we have triune concepts such as the formula, the Spirit is the life, Mind is the builder, and the Physical is the result? The Edgar Cayce readings answer this by saying that man has projected himself into the limitations of a three-dimensional frame of reference. Thus, he will do well in understanding his present state to work with triune concepts.

Our Three-Dimensional Experience

A dimension is simply a mode of measurement. If an experience is multidimensional, then it takes several measurements to describe it accurately. For example, consider a university registrar who wishes to have a means of evaluating or describing a student's educational experience. The registrar might be interested in only two aspects of the student's work: the total number of semester hours completed and the cumulative grade-point average. To this particular registrar, the student's experience is two-dimensional, because all the needed information can be expressed in two measurements.

Man's experience in the earth can best be understood as being three-dimensional. That is, by properly describing three particular measurements, man can evaluate his experiences in the material world. Those three measurements, or dimensions, are time, space, and patience.

Yet, as one finds self as a shadow, or as a representative of that indicated in the eternal—one may ask, what is the source of this association or connection?

It is time, space, and patience that bridges that distance. These are man's concepts of the spirit of God manifesting to the three-dimensional consciousness.   2771-1

. . . Time and Space and Patience in a three-dimensional world are *as* manifestations of Truth into the experiences of souls of men. . .   1463-1

Time is like a blueprint, space is as the manifested building, and patience relates to the purpose for which the building is used.

Viewed from a higher perspective, time has a greater degree of oneness than man, in his three-dimensional consciousness, perceives. It is by the grace of God that we are not forced to meet entirely in one experience all of that which we have built throughout the ages. Instead, the dimension of time enables us to sequentialize our experiences and to work at one time with

3

only a portion of what has been built. Thoughts are things, and step by step, here a little, there a little, we meet ourselves.

How far? How far is tomorrow to any soul? How far is yesterday from thy consciousness?
You are *in* same (that is, all time as one time), yet become gradually aware of it; passing through, then, as it were, God's record or book of consciousness or of remembrance; for meting, being measured out as it were to that to which thou hast attained.   5755-1

Therefore, it is through time that we deal with ideas or thoughts that we have created. These experiences are opportunities for growth; hence, a definition would be "time is the measure of our understanding of an idea."*
Time is the way that man understands or perceives the implications or effects of ideas that he has created, and he does this by sequentializing the experiencing of them—meeting them one after the other and not all at once.

Remember...to him that was given a measure, as a mete, as a rod to measure heaven—as to how large his heaven would be. All right! Then we have as to how much time—What is time? Is it a record merely of the events of self or of the glory of God?...This is as a reckoning. Yet as is shown by the indication of so many days, so many weeks, it is the *inclination* of the individual mind in materiality to set (as was said of John) metes and bounds...   281-33

As these same ideas *manifest* in the material world, we experience them in terms of that dimension called space. Many choose to understand space as being multidimensional in itself (i.e., height, length, and width), yet the readings imply that a more encompassing definition would treat space as a single dimension. Space is always understood in terms of the relationship between objects manifested in the material world. And so, a definition would be "space is the measure of our understanding of a manifested idea."
The third dimension is patience. This is the major lesson that man must learn in his experience in the earth—in time and space. Patience is the awareness that things (effects) are the way they are for a reason (cause) and a purpose. That purpose is that man should come to understand that he is a co-creator and one with God. And so, a definition would be "patience is the

---

*For our understanding of these dimensions, acknowledgement is due J. Everett Irion.

measure of our understanding of the purpose of a manifested idea." Or, as the readings note:

> For to the entity—as to the world—patience is the lesson that each soul must learn in its sojourn through materiality...
> And in patience then does man become more and more aware *of* the continuity of life, of his soul being a portion of the Whole; patience being the portion of man's sphere of activity in the finite being, as time and space manifest the creative and motivative force.
> 1554-3

> Each soul, each entity makes upon time and space—through patience recording same—that as may be indeed the record of the *intent* and *purposes*, as well as the material manifestations of the entity through its sojourn in materiality. [author's italics]
> 1681-1

The emphasis in this third reading should bo placcd upon the relationship of *intent* and *purpose* to patience.

As an illustration of these concepts of time, space, and patience, consider the following story. A mother wished to do something special for her child and had the idea of making a cakc. She decided what ingredients were required and put them on a table in front of her, along with the appropriate mixing bowls and utensils. Then she decided upon the sequence in which she would combine the ingredients. Time is the measure of our understanding of an idea (in this case, the idea of the cake). To the extent that she knew that there were reasons for mixing the ingredients in a certain order, she showed an understanding of and potential mastery of the dimension of time. Her husband may know what those ingredients are, but he does not know the order in which they are to be mixed (that is, the time sequence).

The mother went through the process of making the cake and after an hour it was finished. The cake, which started as an idea, had manifested in space. Space is the measure of our understanding of a *manifested* idea. To the extent that she was able to produce, through application, the finished cake, she showed her understanding and potential mastery of the dimension of space.

But, in the process of making the cake there were many interruptions and the mother accidentally broke a mixing bowl. The entire process became a frustrating thing to her and she began to feel that the child was never appreciative enough of the things that she as a mother did. Seeing the finished cake, the mother was forced to make a decision as to the *purpose* for its manifestation. It could be used to make the child feel guilty for having shown so little appreciation in the past; or, it could

5

be used as an expression of love and joy in the relationship with the child. The lesson that we all have to learn in the earth is patience—the measure of our understanding of the purpose of a manifested idea. To the extent that the mother was patient, she realized that the purpose for the cake was to allow her to express her love.

The Macrocosmic and Microcosmic Trinity

Because we are in a three-dimensional consciousness, we form concepts which are threefold in nature. We experience God and ourselves as triune. Because we are children of God and made in His image, we may conceive of the Godhead as a trinity, with each aspect corresponding to an aspect of the way in which we see ourselves; the Father (the body), the Son (the mind), and the Holy Spirit (the soul).

Ye find thyself—as ye analyze thyself—a body, mind, soul; with a three-dimensional consciousness. Hence ye have a three-dimensional consciousness as related to the earth and to thy heaven, or to thy Godhead. Study the relationship of one to another, for they are one; even as the Father-God is one, but in manifestation—in power and might—has three phases of expression; spirit or soul, mind, and body; Father, Son, and Holy Spirit.   2800-2

Thus as you find in self body, mind, soul, in its three-dimensional manner it is as the spiritual three-dimensional concept of the Godhead; Father, Son, Holy Spirit.
These, then, in self are a shadow of the spirit of the Creative Force. Thus as the Father is as the body, the mind is as the Son, the soul is as the Holy Spirit.   5246-1

As we work with truine concepts we must keep reminding ourselves that the three are actually one. The body, mind and soul are one, just as the Father, Son, and Holy Spirit are merely expressions to man of the One, which is God. We have these three-dimensional concepts because they allow us to function more effectively in our experience in the earth. Each element of the triune concepts meets a particular need in man's search to understand himself.

In the Bible we find a historical illustration of man's evolving understanding of God manifesting in three dimensions, i.e., the macrocosmic Trinity. First came the understanding of the Oneness of God the Father. Then came the understanding of the incarnation of the Spirit in man—the Son. Last came the understanding of the coming of the Holy Spirit—God in all men. At each point of development, which we experience as God's revelation of Himself, a need is met in man's experience, and yet another question or problem is posed. Because of the diversity of his experiences, early man had a concept of many gods, which led to many problems. Our first need was (and is) to learn of His Oneness.

> ...as has ever been the experience of each soul; that the Law is *One*, the Source is *One!* and those that seek other than that find tribulation, turmoils, confusion. 1297-1

This first stage of understanding of the Oneness of God, the Father, is demonstrated by the insights of the Old Testament Israelites who believed in the concept of the One God. "Know, O Israel, the Lord, thy God, is One." (Deut. 6:4) Man, in his experiences in the earth, needs an understanding of the Godhead as being beyond his personal ego. As the work of God is done through us, we must be careful or our egos will claim the credit. Jesus handled this problem with the insight He expressed in saying:

> [One] asked him, Good Master, what shall I do that I may inherit eternal life? And Jesus said unto him, Why callest thou me good? There is none good but one, that is, God. Mark 10:17-18

> ...the Father that dwelleth in me, he doeth the works.
> John 14:10

Yet the concept of oneness is easily misunderstood by man. Because of our limited insight, one, or oneness, implies for us a thing. When we think "oneness," it means a spatial togetherness, implying an object. From this limited viewpoint, the concept of oneness leads to a notion of God as a Being having a locus or residing in some particular place. Since we find evil in the earth, we think God must be outside of our earthly experiences. In other words, the concept of *one* God leads to an impression of God as being transcendent (outside this world) and not immanent (in the midst of human affairs).

This second problem—that of the immanence in addition to the transcendence of the Godhead—is answered in the concept of God, the Son. This second aspect of the Trinity meets the need in man's experience to understand that God is not just out there somewhere, but that He can manifest in fullness among men. Historically this is demonstrated in the life of Jesus, Immanuel, God with us.

Yet Jesus' appearance created a third problem for man in his attempt to understand the Godhead. It became a temptation to think that the full expression of God in the earth could and had happened only through this one individual. Yet He did not call us servants, but brothers:

> For it became him, for whom are all things, and by whom are all things, in bringing many sons into glory, to make the captain of their salvation perfect through sufferings. For both he that sanctifieth and they who are sanctified are all of one: for which cause he is not ashamed to call them brethren, saying, I will declare thy name unto my brethren...
>
> Hebrews 2:10-12
> see also Ps. 22:22

Jesus also said, "These things I have spoken to you while I am still with you. But the Counselor, the Holy Spirit, whom the Father will send in my name, he will teach you all things, and bring to your remembrance all that I have said to you." (John 14:25-26) If Jesus had remained with His disciples they would not have been forced to look within themselves and discover the third expression of the Godhead, which is God, the Holy Spirit.

> Nevertheless I tell you the truth; it is expedient for you that I go away; for if I go not away, the Comforter will not come unto you; but if I depart, I will send him unto you.
>
> John 16:7

By the way, this teaching of Jesus is the answer to any question about the necessity of a guru, or "living master," in the sense of a master presently incarnate in a physical body. The potential for the development of man's understanding of the Godhead is contained within himself, and its realization is not dependent upon another incarnate individual. In John 16: 7 Jesus suggests that the very presence of a divine incarnation works against man's development of the awareness of the Spirit within—"for if I go not away, the Comforter will not come unto you." The invitation to the Comforter to come is the spirit of meditation!

Now let us review man's need for a triune concept of the One God. This may be thought of as a summary of hundreds of years of theological arguments. There is one God, but oneness may be experienced in too limited a way, implying a spatial locus. Since evil is experienced in the earth, God will be placed outside, in a transcendent location in space, and thus it will be imagined that He can have no input or effect on our lives. A corrective to this was the historical incarnation of God in Jesus, which showed that God works in specific and historical ways in the earth. However, the greatness of this incarnation of Immanuel still leads many Christians to forget the aspect of Jesus' work which was to teach us that the Spirit of God will work through us in the same way. Thus the triune concept helps us understand how God can be One yet omnipresent, and "out there" yet manifesting in specific ways in the earth and always "within" our own being.

The following table summarizes the triune relationships suggested thus far:

Macrocosmic	Microcosmic		Dimension	Definition
Holy Spirit	Spiritual	Soul	Patience	The purpose of the manifested idea
Son	Mental	Mind	Time	The idea, form, pattern
Father	Physical (the Whole)	Body	Space	The manifested idea

The Pattern for the Manifestation of God in the Earth

All of these three-dimensional concepts are tools for man. It is by using these tools that man comes to know and experience the oneness behind them. Our purpose for being in the earth is not so much to return to God, but rather to bring the full manifestation of God *into* the three-dimensional consciousness and application. Lama Govinda writes in *Foundations of Tibetan Mysticism:*

> Edwin Arnold's "Light of Asia" ends with the words: "The dew drop slips into the shining sea." If this beautiful simile is reversed, it would probably come nearer to the Buddhist conception of ultimate realization: it is not the dew drop that slips into the sea, but the sea that slips into the drop!

The readings state this principle thus:

> Hence, in the fruits of that—as is given oft, as the fruits of the spirit—does man become aware of the infinite penetrating, or interpenetrating the activities of all forces of matter, or that which is a manifestation of the realm of the infinite into the finite—and the finite becomes conscious of same.   262-52

Our work in the earth, then, is to become One, and thus one with God, by integrating the activities of the body, mind, and

9

soul. When this harmony is attained, there is an attunement that allows God to manifest in His fullness through us. In this context, meditation may be defined as:

...the attuning of the mental body and the physical body to its spiritual source.   281-41

It may accurately be said that when Edgar Cayce was giving a reading he was in meditation, because his ability to give readings was a result of the harmony that existed among these three aspects of himself.

Q-1. . . .please give at this time a term which will best describe Edgar Cayce and his ability to give "readings."
A-1. Application of the harmonious triune. . .It is the harmony of the triune—of body, mind, and soul—towards the purpose of being a help, an assistance, an aid to others.
                                                      254-108

However, the concept that God can express through man is a highly emotionally charged subject. Throughout history, claims that God was manifesting Himself in some way in the earth have both confused man and made him anxious. Some find it especially difficult to comprehend the idea that God can manifest as man.

Philip said to him, "Lord, show us the Father, and we shall be satisfied." Jesus said to him, "Have I been with you so long, and yet you do not know me, Philip? He who has seen me has seen the Father; how can you say, 'Show me the Father'? Do you not believe that I am in the Father and the Father in me?"   John 14:8-10

Others resist the concept entirely and are made so anxious by it that they would destroy those who make such claims. In the following text, the accusation of blasphemy may be interpreted psychologically as anxiety. Such a response stems from man's unwillingness to accept the responsibility for manifesting the Godhead within himself.

"I and the Father are one." [We] took up stones again to stone him. Jesus answered them, "I have shown you many good works from the Father; for which of these do you stone me?" [We] answered him, "We stone you for no good work but for blasphemy; because you, being a man, make yourself God." Jesus answered them, "Is it not written in your law, 'I said, you are gods'?"

John 10:30-34
see also Ps. 82:6

What Jesus came to do was to reawaken within us the knowledge of our divine nature and origin, and remind us of our capacity to become attuned to God, or the Universal Forces. What does this full manifestation of God in three dimensions look like? It appears as the *life of love* in relation to others. It is the fulfillment of the *law of love*, which is *giving*. One reading asks,

...who was the greatest? He that made the worlds or He that washed His disciples' feet? 254-55

The implication is that He was at least as great when He humbled Himself and performed this act of service as He was in the great act of creation.

In the following text, we are invited to this same consciousness and encouraged to claim our divinity as co-creators with Him, yet to manifest that divinity in the earth plane in obedient, humble service. Note the emphasis on having the *mind* of Christ.

Have this *mind* among yourselves, which you have in Christ Jesus, who, though he was in the form of God, did not count equality with God a thing to be grasped, but emptied himself taking the form of a servant, being born in the likeness of men. Philippians 2:5-7 (R.S.V.)

When we have the mind of Christ and are obedient to the Spirit, we manifest in *love:*

... as indicated in the spirit of love, it is universal and gives and takes; is patient, is kind, is forbearing, shows brotherly love.
For it is only in such that one becomes, in materiality, aware of the closeness of relationship to the Creative Forces or God. 1703-3

Q-42. What is the law of love?
A-42. Giving. As is given in this injuction, "Love thy neighbor as thyself." As is given in the injunction, "Love the Lord thy God with all thine heart, thine soul and thine body"...The gift, the giving, with hope of reward or pay is direct opposition of the law of love ...
So we have *love* is *law, law is love. God is love. Love is God.* In that we see the law manifested, not the law itself...Now, if we, as individuals, upon the earth plane, have all of the other elementary forces that make to the bettering of life, and have not love we are as nothing—nothing. 3744-4

Where do we look for this God who can manifest through us? The temptation is constantly to seek outside our own being; but

11

the pattern has been written in our own minds from the
beginning.

> But this is the covenant which I will make with the
> house of Israel after those days, says the Lord: I will put
> my law within them, and I will write it upon their
> hearts; and I will be their God and they shall be my
> people. Jeremiah 31:33 (R.S.V.)

> Go not outside, return into thyself: Truth dwells in the
> inward man. St. Augustine,
> *Liber de vera religione, xxix (72)*

Man does not need to appeal to an external guide or angel or
an external intermediary to obtain knowledge about God for
him. If we rely upon someone else to make contact with God for
us, then we have forgotten the nature of our own being, the
major mission of Jesus, and the deepest wish of God for us—to
be companions with Him.

> But the righteousness based on faith says, Do not say
> in your heart, "Who will ascend into heaven?" (that is,
> to bring Christ down) or "Who will descend into the
> abyss?" (that is, to bring Christ up from the dead) But
> what does it say? The word is near you, on your lips and
> in your heart. Romans 10:6-8 (R.S.V.)

Q-9. How can I increase my strength of mind and body?
**A-9. By resting more and more in Him and meeting Him the
more often in the tabernacle of thine inner being. For He has
promised to meet thee within thine own inner self. And as ye
open thy mind, thy body, thy soul, ye will find Him there; not in
some other place, not as from without. For He is closer than
thyself. For He would be thy very self.** *Meditate* **upon Him and
what He would have thee do.** 833-1

The fundamental concepts of the nature of man are: that we,
being God's children, are spiritual beings, made in His image
and manifesting in three dimensions; and that we therefore
have those attributes of the divine Father, Son and Holy Spirit
in our own bodies, minds and souls. Meditation is attuning the
physical and the mental to the spiritual.

Chapter Two

THE NATURE OF THE MIND

The Spirit is the Life means that there is only one force and that everything that exists is a manifestation of that force. It has many vibrational levels, many qualities or densities; but it is pure energy, and it has as its deepest qualities those of life and of love. Man is a spiritual being and has access to this energy. The soul of man can be described as being made up of three attributes: the mind, the will, and the spirit. It is with the mind that man works with this energy of the spirit, and it is with the will that he chooses how he will work with the mind. That spirit which is a part of our being is one with the Spirit that pervades all of creation. We may represent man's soul as a circle, but that aspect related to the spirit is universal and infinite, and therefore must be represented as being open-ended.

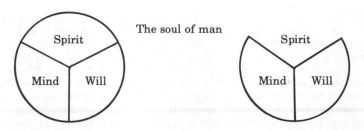

The soul of man

Q-2. With whose spirit, mentioned in the Apostles' Creed, would we commune; with ourselves or God's?
A-2. Within ourselves to God. For, as intimated elsewhere, "My Spirit beareth witness with thy spirit." Whose spirit? There is only *one* Spirit—of Truth. There may be divisions, as there may be many drops of water in the ocean, yet they are all of the ocean. 262-87

What then *is* thy mind? The gift of God, that is the companion with thy soul, that is a part of same! Then if ye would develop that by its use, by its application, it is ministering good and goodness; not for self. 826-11

These are in the experience of each soul. And what the entity does about that free will that is the heritage of each soul, as its *birthright*—the *will*—makes for development or retardment; and nothing may separate thee from the knowledge of the Father but thyself!   1219-1

Mind is the builder. Any time this one energy is expressed in the physical world, it will have qualities of form; it will take on a pattern, shape or vibration. It is the mind that gives the energy its pattern.

It will be found that all have their place; for, as we have given, every force—in its manifestation—is from the One, or God. And that which is manifested in material things is a result, and not the motive force; for mind, mental (which may not be seen with the eye as termed in the material world, but with the spiritual eye) is the builder.   347-2

For mind is the builder, and that entertained, that builded, that pattern set in same is that to which the body, the mind and the soul attains by this constancy held before same.   370-3

As the one energy is given a form, we can begin to speak of it objectively, for a thought is a thing! The mental activity called desire creates from the one energy a vibrational pattern that has an objective reality:

. . . for, as in energy, there is seen the relativity of space and force as is begun, and as same continues to vibrate, that one law remains. Whenever it vibrates in the *same* vibration, it shows as the same thing. That's deep for you, yes. But when time, space, and the effect of thought and the activity of same— same was given aforetime through the Master, in this: "Your law says that he that committeth adultery shall be stoned, but *I* say he that looketh on a woman to *lust* after her has committed adultery already." Now here we have relativity of force as applied through the mental body. Here we have as in application of same to the various experiences in the earth's plane and application of, when taking thought, or building by the mental body, this contributed or detracted from the soul of the individual.   254-47

For, thoughts are things! and they have their effect upon individuals, especially those that become supersensitive to outside influences! These are just as physical as sticking a pin in the hand!   386-2

. . . for thoughts are deeds and may be miracles or crimes in their execution and the end thereof.   5680-1

14

And so, mind is the mediator between this pure, life-giving energy and its manifestation—between the spirit and the physical. It is with the mind that we can modify the way that this energy is expressed in the earth. As the mediator, the mind partakes of both that which is temporal and that which is eternal—of the finite nature of the physical body and the infinite nature of the soul. Referring to this same principle, Lama Govinda writes:

> Manas [mind] is that element of our consciousness which holds the balance between the empirical-individual qualities on the one side and the universal-spiritual qualities on the other. It is that which either binds us to the world of the senses or which liberates us from it. *(Foundations of Tibetan Mysticism, p. 75)*

Our work in being in the earth is to bring the Spirit into manifestation in the three-dimensional world. Therefore, because it is the mediator between the spiritual and the physical, the mind can be understood as the Way. It is through the mind that our work is accomplished. In relationship to the Trinity, the mind corresponds to the Son or the savior. Through the activity of the mind, attuned to the spirit within, man is saved from the belief in his separation from God. If our future life is salvation—a movement beyond this worldly state of consciousness—then what we have built with the mind determines where we will go in consciousness.

For, the body and its soul is hinged upon the mental. For, in material manifestation in a three-dimensional world, mind is the builder and represents that which is the experience of most entities, the Son, in the Godhead, or man's concept of same.
2850-1

Q-2. Where do I go from this planet?
A-2. Where thou art preparing, and what thou art building.
1219-1

Then the Master—as the mind—is the way, is the how, that one becomes aware through application, through administration of the hopes, the desires, the faith of the soul itself. For, mind is of the body and of soul, and when purified in the Christ Consciousness it lives on and on as such. 3292-1

Thoughts are food for the physical body and the soul. That which the mind dwells upon will manifest in the physical—either immediately or lifetimes afterward—for it has become a part of the soul as well. This is a highly significant principle with respect to meditation. When we enhance our access to the

15

one creative energy through meditation, what the mind is going to do with this energy becomes extremely important. That which we hold in the mind we tend to become; that which we hold in the mind during meditation we become, even more surely. If we hold something negative, we allow this energy to flow through us and manifest that negativity in the physical. If we dwell upon anger, we are meditating, in a manner of speaking, and we build that into our being.

Then that our mind dwells upon, that our mind feeds upon, that do we supply to our body—yes, to our soul! 1567-2

The transmigration of life takes place in one's mind. Let one therefore keep the mind pure, for what a man thinks, that he becomes.   *Upanishads*

For as he thinketh in his heart, so is he. . .
Prov. 23:7 (KJV)

Vibration and Dimensions as Mediating Concepts

In order to understand how one kind of stuff, the one force of the spirit, can interact with another kind of stuff, that which we call matter, we need some mediating concepts. Mind is essentially the mediator between the spiritual and the physical. There are other concepts that are helpful in understanding these interrelationships. One way to think of the mind as the builder is to think of it as imparting a vibrational pattern and frequency to the energy. When the energy of the one force is given specific vibrational patterns and relationships, as in the makeup of an atom, we may think of the energy as having projected into materialization. What is the difference between energy and matter? The vibrational pattern and frequency.

Another mediating concept that may help us to sense the oneness between matter and the pure energy of the Spirit is the concept of planes or dimensions. These can also be thought of as different vibrational frequencies. We have discussed the three-dimensional nature of our present consciousness, yet the readings say that there are eight dimensions in the solar system, corresponding to the planets from Mercury to Neptune. In the three-dimensional state of consciousness of the earth it is difficult for us to comprehend fully the meaning of dimensions beyond our own. Yet some information was given concerning the nature of these other dimensions—particularly the fourth dimension. There is a strong parallel between the

16

understanding given in the Edgar Cayce readings and that of the writings of the Swiss psychologist, C.G. Jung. Compare these definitions:

> If we wish to form a vivid picture of a non-spatial being of the fourth dimension, we should do well to take *thought as a being* for our model.
> *(Modern Man in Search of a Soul,* p. 184)

Best definition that ever may be given of fourth dimension is an idea! Where will it project? Anywhere! Where does it arise from? Who knows! Where will it end? Who can tell! It is all inclusive! It has both length, breadth, height, depth—is without beginning and is without ending! 364-10

As an illustration of these concepts let us consider a book. What is real about a book? Is it the cover, the paper, or the type of print used? Rather, the ideas expressed or contained within the book constitute its power and its deeper reality. The ideas— the fourth-dimensional qualities—have a more permament effect upon us than does the physical appearance.

First—one finds self in a three-dimensional plane of consciousness; all that may be known materially is subject to that dimension.
That as may be comprehended in the mental may reach into a fourth-dimensional plane—as the variation between a book with its dimension and the contents of same, which may be of a mental reaction entirely. 1861-4

The three-dimensional world can be understood as a projection of the fourth dimension. The principle here is that when something is projected it takes on a lesser dimension. For example, consider the situation in which a man shines a flashlight on a basketball in such a way that the shadow of the ball appears as a two-dimensional area—a darkened circle on the wall. In a similar manner, the readings say that everything we perceive in our three-dimensional world is simply a projection of the fourth dimension, which is the realm of thoughts or ideas.

The abilities in the *psychic* forces. . .psychic meaning, then, of the mental *and* the soul—doesn't necessarily mean the body, until it's enabled to be brought *into* being in whatever form it may make its manifestation—which may never be in a material world, or take form in a three-dimensional plane as the earth is; it may remain in a fourth-dimensional—which is an idea! 364-10

17

Truly then do thoughts become the deeds, and find, as in this, the manifestation in the different manners in the life of each... truly is there found that the desire must precede the action and that directed thought becomes action in the concrete manner, through each force that the spiritual element manifests through. And there then becomes the three manifestations in the three manners, in the three ways, all projections from a fourth-dimensional condition into a third-dimensional mind.   106-9

From this point of view, the readings say that consciousness as we know it is a past condition. What we see as our material world is the result of mental processes that have taken place previously.

Q-4. Explain. "So those things that do appear to have reality, and their reality to the human mind, have in reality passed into past conditions before they have reached the mind, for with the earth's laws and its relation to other spheres has man become a past condition."
A-4. This relates to that of the spiritual law in its relative forces in the earth planes, or that of a finite mind attempting to comprehend the laws of the infinite mind. For, before *any* condition exists in the finite mind [three-dimensional consciousness], it has become a past condition, relatively spoken, from the infinite mind.   900-24

What appears as form does thus belong essentially to the past, and is therefore felt as alien by those who have developed spiritually beyond it.(Lama Govinda, p. 69)

That which we experience now as reality is in actuality the manifestation of what we have built previously. Our thought patterns are analogous to the blueprints of an architect. Once the blueprint has been drawn, we know what the building will look like when it manifests. It is only a matter of transforming it from the idea level into physical manifestation. We can go back and modify our thought patterns—modify the blueprints—but unless we do, the nature of the manifestation is determined or fixed. The readings say that nothing of importance happens in our lives without being foreshadowed in a dream, because in the dream state we can tune in to that blueprint level and see what we are building. Fourth-dimensional reality, therefore, is the level at which the process of building is taking place. Once something manifests in the three-dimensional world, it is a past condition, relatively speaking.

18

Often we may try to force conditions to change at the material level without appreciating the fact that the real change must come at the mental or idea level. Such a misunderstanding is likely to lead to frustration in relationships with others or with social institutions. In the principle stated below, we can understand what Lama Govinda calls "the process of formation" to take place at the creative level of thought.

Materialization can be influenced, directed and modified only while it is still in the process of formation.
(Lama Govinda, p. 214)

How does the one energy move from beyond the four-dimensional level of thought or idea through to the three-dimensional level of manifestation? We may use the concept of *vibrations* of finer and coarser densities as mediating between the realities of the different dimensions. An analogy can be drawn between the dimensions and the three different vibrational or energy levels of water: Water as a gas can be compared with the spiritual level, beyond the fourth dimension; liquid water would then relate to the mind and the fourth dimension; and water in the solid state would correspond to physical manifestations in the earth.

Process and Structure

Just as man has a triune concept of the Godhead and of himself, he perceives three levels of mind activity—conscious, subconscious and superconscious—and three bodies—physical, mental, and spiritual. The spiritual body is the soul. In each case, the three are only manifestations of the one. In order to understand the way in which the readings describe these three levels, it is necessary to differentiate between a "structure" and a "process." A structure is a form or body that has patterned existence in itself; whereas a process is the dynamic relationship that exists between structures. The interaction of two structures creates a process—which in turn may modify one or both of the structures. Consider the nations of the world as individual structures and the negotiations, treaties and trade agreements as processes among these structures. Each of these processes can potentially affect the nature of the structures. A trade agreement, for example, may drastically alter the economic system of a nation.

Man, with his three-dimensional consciousness, sees himself as comprising three structures—a physical body, a mental body, and a soul body.

Each soul, individual or entity, finds these facts existent:

There is the body-physical—with all its attributes for the functioning of the body in a three-dimensional or a manifested earth plane.

Also there is the body-mental—which is that directing influence of the physical, the mental and the spiritual emotions and manifestations of the body; or the way, the manner in which conduct is related to self, to individuals, as well as to things, conditions and circumstances. While the mind may not be seen by the physical senses, it can be sensed by others; that is, others may sense the conclusions that have been drawn by the body-mind of an individual, by the manner in which such an individual conducts himself in relationship to things, conditions or people.

Then there is the body-spiritual, or soul body—that eternal something that is invisible. It is only visible to that consciousness in which the individual entity in patience becomes aware of its relationship to the mental and the physical being.

All of these then are one—in an entity; just as it is considered, realized or acknowledged that the body, mind and soul are one—that God, the Son and the Holy Spirit are one.   2475-1

[The physical body is] That which is of the earth-earthy; that channel, that house, that piece of clay that is motivated in material forces as the dwelling place of the spirit or the soul ...

The soul body is the motivative power within, that has either grown in the constructive forces in its associations or activities, or to the gratifying, satisfying of the superficial emotions or urges.   262-85

Relating to the mental body and those reactions in the imaginative functionings through which ideas or ideals may be formed, as in this body, there may be quite a dissertation given respecting what the mental body really is, or how it may be called a body at all:

There are organs; there are arteries; there are veins, nervous systems, along which it may be said that the mental body functions as for its manifestation in materiality. Yet no one outside of a body may be able to tell what another body thinks or feels by watching, measuring, testing, in any form or manner, those reactions to the organs, veins and various conditions in activity to give expression.

Hence, being in such relationships to that which is both physical *and* material—and spiritual—it may be well said there *is* a body.   276-7

The following diagram gives a summary of the relationships among the three bodies:

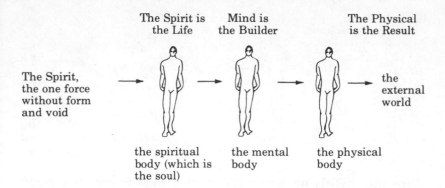

The Spirit is the Life   Mind is the Builder   The Physical is the Result

The Spirit, the one force without form and void → the spiritual body (which is the soul) → the mental body → the physical body → the external world

Consciousness is the relationship between any two neighboring structures. It is a process; it does not exist as a thing in and of itself within the physical body, the mental body or the soul body. This principle is demonstrated in the following two readings.

For, as may be said, *desire* is that impulse which makes for the activity of the mental body. . .   276-7

Q-2. If cremated, would the body feel it?
A-2. What body? The physical body is not the consciousness. The consciousness of the physical body is a separate thing. There is the mental body, the physical body, the spiritual body...
As to how long it requires to lose physical consciousness depends upon how great are the *appetites* and desires of a physical body!   1472-2

The first reading attributes desire to the mental body; the second makes it clear that physical consciousness is not simply within the physical body. Instead, physical consciousness should be understood as the relationship between the physical body and desire (which is of the mental body). Consciousness is a process—a relationship between two structures.

The readings define three levels of consciousness. First is the conscious, which is directly related to those processes involving the physical body. These processes are: (1) the relationship between the external world and the physical body, which operates through the five senses; (2) the relationships between sub-structures within the physical body, which create the conscious awareness of internal activity (e.g., the relationship between the brain and stomach that creates the awareness that one is hungry); and (3) the relationship between the physical body and the mental body, which appears as imagination or daydreaming within the conscious mind.

21

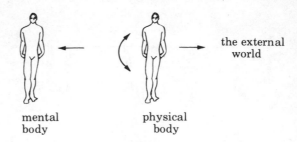

the processes of
conscious awareness

mental
body

the external
world

physical
body

For the earthly or material consciousness is ever tempered with material conditions. . .In the consciousness of earthly or material forces there enters all the attributes of the physical, fleshly body. 900-16

Knowledge comes through the senses in the physical body to the conscious mind. 900-21

Definition of the words "conscious mind":
The *conscious* means *that* that is able to be manifested in the physical plane through one of the senses. 3744-1

The second level of consciousness is the subconscious, which comprises those processes involving the mental body. Specifically, these would be the relationships between the soul and the mental body (e.g., subconscious awareness of past-life experiences) and between the physical body and the mental body (e.g., dreams relating to the physical body).

the processes of
subconscious awareness

spiritual
body

mental
body

physical
body

The subconscious. . .[partakes] then of the soul forces, and of the material plane, as acted upon through and by mental mind [i.e., the mental body]. 900-31

Finally, there is the superconscious mind, which is defined as the relationship between the soul and the Spirit.

22

the process of
the superconscious

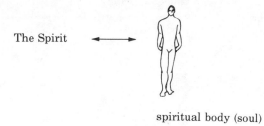

The Spirit ←——→

spiritual body (soul)

...the superconsciousness with the consciousness between
soul and spirit, and partakes of the spiritual forces principally.
900-16

The superconscious is the divide, that oneness lying between
the soul and the spirit force, within the spiritual entity. Not of
earth forces at all, only awakened with the spiritual
indwelling and acquired individually. 900-21

It is only as physical consciousness is laid aside that the
superconscious can have a *direct* effect on man's experience. As
physical consciousness is released (as in sleep and that called
death), the subconscious becomes the conscious and the
superconscious becomes the subconscious.
In meditation man seeks to attune himself to the
superconscious; thus it is only by stilling the conscious (the
senses, the physical) and the subconscious (the mental) that he
is able to make this movement in awareness to a point where
the superconscious is more accessible.

The superconscious mind being that of the spiritual entity,
and in action only when the subconscious is become the
conscious mind. 900-31

For, as we find in the spiritual entity the subconscious, in the
physical world it becomes the conscious; in the spiritual that
known in the physical as the superconscious becomes the
subconscious. 900-23

These processes or relationships, which man experiences as
levels of consciousness, can be illustrated by the following
diagram.

23

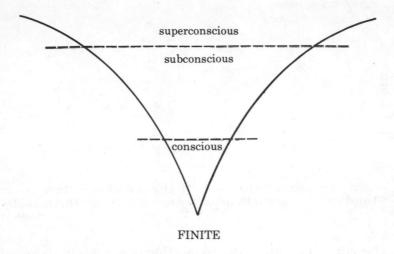

INFINITE

superconscious

subconscious

conscious

FINITE

Here we can see that consciousness is only a small fraction of the potential of our total being.

Our normal waking consciousness, rational consciousness as we call it, is but one special type of consciousness, whilst all about it, parted from it by the filmiest of screens, there lie potential forms of consciousness entirely different. . .No account of the universe in its totality can be final which leaves these other forms of consciousness quite disregarded. . .they forbid a premature closing of our accounts with reality. (William James, *The Varieties of Religious Experience* quoted in *Passages: A Guide for Pilgrims of the Mind.* Harper & Row, N.Y., 1972, p. 15.)

Man in the earth is but a finite focal point of consciousness. Lying, as it were, just beyond man's physical, waking consciousness is the subconscious. Here are stored the memory patterns of all that man has thought and experienced. To the degree that these patterns are of a limiting or selfish nature, they constitute barriers to the flow of energy and information from the superconscious. The superconscious is that level of awareness which is fully attuned to God. At this level there is an understanding of the fundamental oneness that pervades all of creation. It is here, in the mind of the soul, that there is written that pattern of perfection, the awareness of our true nature as spiritual beings.

This is the covenant that I will make with them after
those days, saith the Lord, I will put my laws into their
hearts, and in their minds I will write them.

Hebrews 10:16

With this understanding of the nature of the mind, we may
reconsider and redefine meditation.

Since man is a child of God and was created in His image, we
bear within us a pattern of perfection, of oneness with the One.
That pattern is written within us, in our hearts and in our
minds. Yet it is a potential, residing dormant like a seed.

In meditation, we awaken that pattern by setting it as the
spiritual ideal, stilling the physical and the mental from their
ordinary pursuits, directing them with an affirmation that
expresses the spiritual ideal, and inviting the energy of the
Spirit to flow through the pattern and into the fullness of our
being. When the mind, as the builder, dwells upon the pattern of
the Godhead within and we make it authentic through
application, we become that pattern. We were created in His
image and we may thus become, as we were destined to become,
"conformed to the image of His Son." (Romans 8:29)

Thus we define meditation as "the attuning of the mental
body and the physical body to its spiritual source." (281-41)

Chapter Three

PHYSIOLOGY OF MEDITATION

One of the most important insights to be gained from the Edgar Cayce readings on meditation is that it is not just a spiritual exercise. It involves the body and the mind as well. In this chapter we shall examine some specific events that take place in the body as we enter into deep meditation.

A problem that has perplexed philosophers and theologians for hundreds of years can be stated as follows: If there is, in fact, an infinite spiritual dimension to our being, how is it able to contact or affect our finite physical nature? Another way of phrasing this question might be: Where does the life force or the divine force touch the body? Or, how does the soul interact with the body? It is interesting to consider from a historical perspective where man has thought life is located. At some periods he has felt that life is in the heart. At other times, in the liver. In our day the tendency is to think of life as being in the head or the cortex of the brain. However, a very important concept from the readings is that life touches the body in every cell. We are trying to awaken in meditation an awareness of the life force that is going to affect the entire body, not just the thoughts in the brain.

To answer the question of how the infinite is able to affect the finite, the readings begin with the concept that the body is the temple—not only in the sense of a temple as a place, but also as an edifice specially constructed for optimally fulfilling a specific function. The readings on meditation reveal an exciting and beautiful picture of the way in which man is *purposefully* constructed to enable him to be a companion with God in awareness, knowledge and energy. The human body is potentially a very special kind of instrument that provides distinct channels for tuning in to the infinite energy and enabling it to express itself in the material world. In the following two readings we find reference to the way in which the body responds in deep meditation.

26

... there are *definite* conditions that arise from within the inner man when an individual enters into true or deep meditation. A physical condition happens, a physical activity takes place! Acting through what? Through that man has chosen to call the imaginative or the impulsive ...   281-13

... there are physical contacts which the anatomist finds not, or those who would look for imaginations or the minds. Yet it is found that within the body there are channels, there are ducts, there are glands, there are activities that perform no one knows what! in a living, *moving,* thinking being. 281-41

The "physical contacts" and "glands" referred to here are the endocrine system. Physiologists note that the glands are the miracle workers of the body; we know them personally to be closely related to our emotions—e.g., the adrenals relate to anger. The readings are saying that when the endocrine glands become properly attuned, they become spiritual centers and points of contact through which energy and information can flow from God to man.

A word that describes the way in which these glands or spiritual centers function is "transduction." This is not a word that Edgar Cayce used, but it seems to be an effective one for summarizing the concept that is in the readings. It is a word that is frequently used by physiologists. A transducer is a device that takes energy from one system and provides energy in a different form to another system. For example, a telephone is a transducer. It takes electrical energy and transforms it into sound waves. Let us now look at this definition in terms of the two primary systems of our own being—our infinite nature and our finite nature. We could illustrate the concept of transducers in the following way:

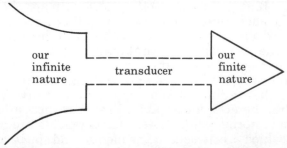

our infinite nature — transducer — our finite nature

The readings suggest that there are seven very special contact points or transducers within the body that have an important relationship to our spiritual nature. Where are those transducers and what are they? They have been talked about for thousands of years. In the East they are called the chakras; in the Edgar Cayce readings they are referred to as spiritual centers. Many people who are consciously psychic claim to be able to see things that are not visible to the normal person's eye; they say that they can see energy patterns or vortices of energy that touch the body in seven places. There seems to be a general agreement among various people as to where these points of contact are: (1) in the forehead, (2) at the top of the head, (3) in the throat region, (4) in the area of the heart, (5) at the solar plexus, (6) in the lower abdomen, and (7) in the groin area, or at the base of the spine. Sometimes these centers have been drawn in the East as touching the spine, running from its base up to the top of the head.

The information in Edgar Cayce's readings about the spiritual centers most frequently refers to them in terms of the endocrine glands. There is one endocrine gland for each of the spiritual centers. We can imagine the endocrine system to be a set of seven fabulous jewels of different colors. That system is primarily composed of the following seven centers: pituitary, pineal, thyroid, thymus, adrenal, cells of Leydig, and gonads. The functioning of these ductless glands, secreting their numerous hormones directly into the blood stream, is unimaginably complex. We can visualize this system as being like a symphony orchestra. Properly attuned and functioning in a harmonious and integrated way as a single system, it produces magnificent music, a hymn of the universe that lifts us from the finite into attunement with the infinite. Or, think of this system as being like a seven-piece band. One or two instruments may step forward and "solo" while the others continue to play in the background; on occasion, one of the players may hog the show and usurp the role of the others.

In our consideration of the spiritual centers you must remember that the center itself is more than just the endocrine gland. For each center there is also a gathering of nerves in the area, called a plexus, and we might think of the plexus as being a part of the overall activity that makes up the spiritual center. For example, with the thymus there is also the cardiac plexus, the heart as the heart center, and the lungs as the air center. In addition, the readings would suggest, and many clairvoyants agree, that there are energy fields in each of these areas that are invisible to normal sight. These energy fields are parts of the centers, which are present in the mental and spiritual bodies as well as in the physical. These glands, with their associated nerve plexuses and energy fields, work together to create a complex of activity focused in seven places, which can be symbolized as churches, in the body.

The teaching in the readings is that these spiritual centers are the transducers between our spiritual nature and our finite physical nature. The soul is able to have a physical effect through these transducers. These centers are always operative, but they are usually in a state of dis-ease or lack of harmony, and thus are not working together for optimum healing and attunement. In meditation we are seeking to awaken the activities of these centers, not separately, but as a system, so that they function in their highest, most integrative way.

Three Correlate Systems

There are three important systems which are the physiological bases of our experiences in meditation. These three have a one-to-one relationship with the three levels of mind: conscious, subconscious and superconscious. The first of these systems is the part of the cerebrospinal system that is under our conscious control. This is related especially to the five senses and muscular actions, and it corresponds to the physical body and the conscious mind. For example, we use the cortex of our brain and the spinal cord to carry nerve impulses to various muscles when we consciously decide to make some movement.

The second system is the autonomic system, which corresponds to the subconscious mind. The autonomic system controls automatic subconscious functioning; for example, your heartbeat, breathing or digestion.

The third system is the endocrine system, which has a special relationship to the soul and the superconscious mind.

If we are to meditate, we have to make use of that part of the cerebrospinal system that is under our conscious control to make the effort of giving the proper time to meditation. If we are sitting in front of the television, it takes will power and conscious effort to get up and turn the set off and get ourselves into another room to meditate. This conscious effort is the first step in the physiology of meditation. Probably in the initial part of our meditation periods we will be using the cerebrospinal system primarily. Under our conscious direction our body goes through preparatory exercises, and the conscious mind is then focused on an affirmation. When we say "effort" is required to focus on an affirmation, we don't want to imply that meditation is straining. Instead, the word "effort" implies the sense of doing it, making it a discipline and directing our conscious will to awaken the joy of doing it each day.

If the conscious effort can quiet the outer body, then, through the autonomic system, we are able to attain a stillness and quiet within the body. There is a distinct part of the autonomic nervous system, called the *parasympathetic nervous system,* that allows the body to relax, to be still and to be quiet.

Laboratory research with various forms of meditation has shown that this relaxation or quieting response takes place naturally as we meditate. As we quiet the sympathetic nervous system and activate the parasympathetic, we awaken processes that are usually inhibited by the frantic and stressful way that we live daily. Once we have attained stillness, the superconscious pattern, which is being awakened by the conscious ideal can express itself in the form of harmonious and integrated functioning within the endocrine system.

A Closer Look at the Spiritual Centers

Now let us examine the types of experiences and qualities of consciousness that may be related to each of the spiritual centers. In addition, we shall examine the location and the function of the endocrine gland related to each center.

The Gonad Center. The gonads are the endocrine glands that correspond to the first spiritual center. In the male these are the testes; in the female, the ovaries. This center has to do with our instinct to seek sustenance. If we think of the true sustenance as the love of God supplying manna, our daily bread, from heaven, we can understand why the Church of Ephesus was told in The Revelation of John to return to its first love. In some Eastern schools of thought, this center is referred to as the root chakra. The gonads qualify as endocrine glands by secreting various of the sex hormones. Symbolically, as in dreams, this center and its activities can be represented by the color red, the element earth, and the archetypal symbolic visions of the bull or calf.

The Cells of Leydig Center. The second center has to do with our experiences related to the male-female balance within us. From the Bible and the readings we know that as spiritual beings we are not really male or female. At the level of the soul, there is a oneness and wholeness which, while we are in bodies and in the earth, we are seeking in the seeming opposites. This wholeness may be sought through sexual activity, but it also may be attained by balancing the masculine and feminine qualities. This center is related to the biological instinct for propagation of the species.

The cells of Leydig are found within the gonads as interstitial cells. They secrete the sex hormone testosterone, a masculinizing hormone that affects the secondary sexual characteristics and is produced in both sexes. In a corresponding way, some slight production of female hormones takes place in the testes. The cells of Leydig are found in greater number in the testes than in the ovaries, in which they may be referred to as the hilus cells.

This center is represented by the color orange, the element water, and the androgynous man as a symbol. In The Revelation, it corresponds to the Church of Smyrna.

The Adrenal Center. The third spiritual center, associated with the adrenal glands, especially relates to our sense of power in the earth and to the instinct for self-preservation. When this center is operating in an integrative fashion with the other centers, it may express itself as courage or persistence, even rarely as righteous indignation. When it is operating in an inharmonious way, we have experiences such as fear or destructive anger. The adrenal glands themselves are most frequently associated with the fight-or-flight instinct. As can be seen in the diagram below, the adrenal glands sit just above the kidneys. They have a far-reaching effect on the various functions of the body.

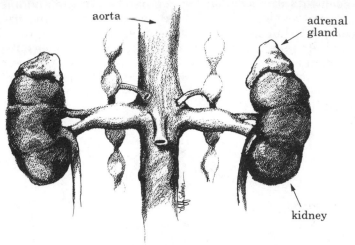

aorta

adrenal gland

kidney

The adrenal gland is constructed as a gland within a gland. The inner part of the adrenal is called the medulla, and it secretes two hormones, adrenaline and nonadrenaline, which are released into the blood when we confront a stressful situation. The outer portion of the adrenal gland is called the adrenal cortex, and it secretes many hormones: sexual hormones, hormones that affect blood sugar level, and hormones that affect the concentration of minerals in the blood.

In this same region of the body is a gathering of nerves, the solar plexus. The third spiritual center, therefore, takes in the operation of the adrenal glands, the activities of the solar plexus nerves, and the higher-vibrational energy fields located in this area of the body. The color that represents this center is yellow, the element is fire, the symbolic animal is the lion, and the Church in The Revelation is Pergamos.

The Thymus Center. The fourth spiritual center has largely to do with our experiences related to love in the earth. Thus it is also related to the instinct for self-gratification. Consider such colloquial phrases as "broken-hearted" and "hard-hearted," which reflect activities or experiences of this fourth center. Maternal love would be an example of the highest expression of the center. In the past 15 years science has begun to understand the thymus gland. It has been found to play a most important role in the body's defense against disease, its immunological system, and is especially concerned with lymphocytes, which make up a part of the white blood cell count. Lymphocytes are manufactured in the thymus, as well as in the lymph nodes, the spleen and areas called Peyer's patches in the abdomen. The thymus can properly be called an endocrine gland because it secretes a hormone that stimulates the production of these lymphocyte cells in the other three areas. As will be noted in the diagram below, the thymus has two lobes and is found directly behind the breastbone. It seems to be most active in children and begins to shrink during adolescence; nevertheless, its functions extend throughout adult life.

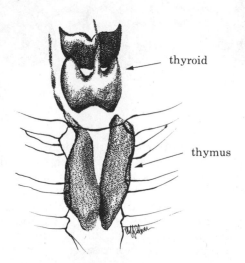

These first four centers relate particularly to our experiences in the earth. They are often referred to as the four lower centers—"lower" in the sense that they are spatially located in the lower part of the body, but also in that they are concerned most frequently with man's survival and expression in the earth.

The remaining three centers are especially related to the potential for awareness of our divine nature. They form a trinity within ourselves. Thus the thymus is like a balancing point between the lower centers and the upper centers. To the degree that our experiences of love are controlled by the three lower centers, that love tends to be selfish, and hence we remain bound to an earthly concept of life. However, if our experiences of love are directed and controlled by the upper three centers, we begin to break free of limited concepts of our being. For this reason, the thymus center is frequently symbolized by a bird such as the eagle, which is able to soar free of earthly limitations. The thymus can also be symbolized by the color green and the element air, which reflects its location near the lungs. The corresponding Church in The Revelation is Thyatira.

The Thyroid Center. As a spiritual center, the thyroid relates to the faculty of the will. When it is operating under the direction of the superconscious pattern, the will is made one with divine will (as expressed, for example, in the affirmation "Not my will, but Thine"). It also relates to the Spirit and may reflect the spirit of obedience, as in Jesus, or the spirit of rebellion. The stubbornness of self-will is described repeatedly in the Bible's references to God's children as a stiff-necked people. Physiologically, this center relates to the thyroid gland, which surrounds the windpipe (as is depicted in the previous diagram). The hormones secreted by this gland control the metabolism rate in the body, or how fast the body uses energy. When the thyroid is not functioning properly, a person may develop a swelling in that area, called a goiter, as the gland tries to readjust. Some malfunctions of this gland lead to profound depression. Another endocrine gland that is adjacent to the thyroid and often considered to be a part of it is the parathyroid. This gland secretes a hormone that controls the level of calcium in the blood.

The color symbolic of the fifth center is blue (or gray), the element is ether, and the Church is Sardis.

The Pineal Center. If we consider the spiritual centers in sequential order, the pineal gland relates to the sixth center, even though spatially it is situated higher in the brain than the pituitary. The pineal center is most often referred to in mystical literature as being the higher mind or the Christ center. Thus it would be related to the experience of Light. As the consciousness of this center is awakened, we achieve conscious access to the records and remembrance of everything that we have ever experienced. For those working with the possibility of reincarnation, it is at this level that past-life memories are available.

Only in the past decade has science come to understand and acknowledge some of the endocrine functions of the pineal gland. Yet, hundreds of years ago, the philosopher Descartes claimed that the pineal was the seat of the soul. He felt that mysterious strands carried impulses from the eyes to the pineal. The pineal then secreted substances that traveled to the muscles and directed them to make appropriate responses to what was being seen. The theory was quickly dropped by medical science; but it is interesting to note that (1) Edgar Cayce suggested that the pineal was closely related to our awareness of ourselves as souls, and (2) medical science has discovered that the pineal is sensitive to light. It is not sensitive quite as directly as Descartes claimed; rather, the impulse takes a roundabout pathway. Most of the nerve impulses from the eye travel along the optic nerve to various portions of the brain. However, there is one small branch that carries the impulse down through the hypothalamus and into the spinal cord. From there, the nerve impulse travels up to the superior cervical

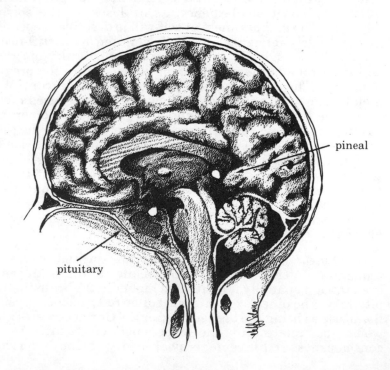

pineal

pituitary

ganglia, and from there it is relayed to the pineal gland. That nerve impulse, which carries information about the light striking the eyes, has a direct effect on the manufacture of a hormone in the pineal.

This insight from medical science is significant in at least two ways. First, it demonstrates that the only known connection between the nervous system and the sixth spiritual center passes through the neck area. Many people have found a simple head and neck exercise (recommended in the readings) an effective preparatory activity before meditation. It is possible that in doing this exercise we are exerting a direct influence upon the pineal gland through these neural connections. A second point, probably more important, relates to the hormone produced by the pineal gland, which is affected by light. This hormone, called melatonin, has been found to have an inhibiting effect upon the hormone secreted by the cells of Leydig, testosterone. This hormonal relationship directly corresponds to the description given in the readings of the movement of energy in meditation. The relationship between the cells of Leydig and the pineal is probably the most important one in the physiology of meditation. The cells of Leydig are a door that may be either sealed or open; the pineal is always the open door. Together they may be said truly to constitute a seat of the soul. In meditation we seek to move the creative energy associated with the cells of Leydig center directly to the pineal center. At that point, the energy is able to take on the qualities of consciousness related to the pineal center (the mind of Christ), and it is then able to overflow into the pituitary and move back down, affecting the functions of the lower centers, healing and integrating our activities. Both the raising and the overflow of the energy may be referred to, as in *The Secret of the Golden Flower*, as the backward-flowing motion.

The color for this sixth center is indigo and the Church is Philadelphia, truly the city of brotherly love.

The Pituitary Center. The quality of consciousness of this highest center is oneness—the awareness of the oneness of all life. Spiritual healing emanates from this center. Actually, in understanding the function of the pituitary, we must consider an adjacent area called the hypothalamus. Not only is the hypothalamus the master control center of the autonomic nervous system, it has a significant controlling influence on the pituitary as well. The pituitary sits in a bony cup surrounded on one side by sinus cavities, and just above it is the hypothalamus.

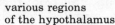

various regions
of the hypothalamus

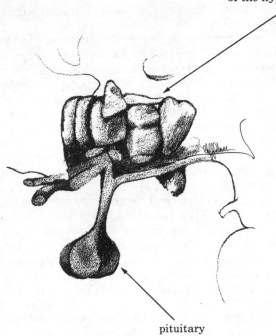

pituitary

The pituitary is made up of two distinct regions, a posterior lobe and an anterior one. The posterior lobe is primarily an extension of nerves from the hypothalamus. At one time it was thought that the posterior lobe synthesized and secreted two hormones, but recently it has been discovered that these hormones are manufactured in the hypothalamus and stored in the posterior lobe of the pituitary before they are released into the blood stream. The anterior lobe of the pituitary is slightly larger and secretes many different types of hormones: those that control the menstrual cycle, the growth hormone, and hormones that affect the functions of the thyroid and adrenals. Because of its effect on all the other glands, the pituitary has been referred to as the master gland. However, this distinction must be shared with the hypothalamus, because nearly all of the pituitary's hormonal secretions are influenced to some degree by this region of the brain directly above it.

The symbolic color for this seventh center is violet and the Church is Laodicea.

A summary of these concepts related to the seven spiritual centers is shown in the following diagram and chart.

36

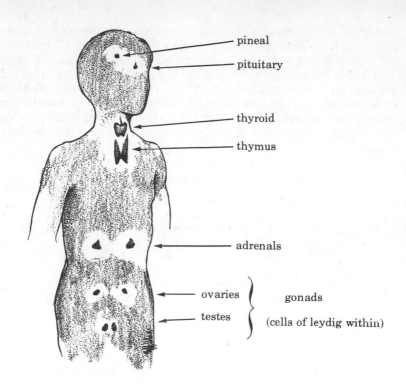

Center	Endocrine Gland	Symbols Color	Element	Image	Revelation Church
1	Gonads	Red	Earth	Bull or calf	Ephesus
2	Cells of Leydig	Orange	Water	Androgynous man	Smyrna
3	Adrenals	Yellow	Fire	Lion	Pergamos
4	Thymus	Green	Air	Eagle	Thyatira
5	Thyroid	Blue	Ether	Spirit (Holy)	Sardis
6	Pineal	Indigo		Son (Christ)	Philadelphia
7	Pituitary	Violet		Father	Laodicea

The Two Primary Functions of the Centers as Transducers

The spiritual centers as transducers have two primary functions, one of which is illustrated by a helpful analogy from the Cayce readings. Think of the spiritual aspect of our being as *light*—the one fundamental energy that is expressing itself in the physical world. Now consider how a slide projector works. It has a bulb which projects light onto a screen. The other essential component, of course, is a slide, the image or pattern that this light activates and projects onto the screen. This is one way of understanding the relationship between spirit, mind and body: the light of the spirit shines through a pattern (of consciousness) and manifests as a projection (our physical experience). It is also a good analogy for demonstrating how these spiritual centers are both the gatherers of spiritual energy and the storehouses of patterns of consciousness that we have built.

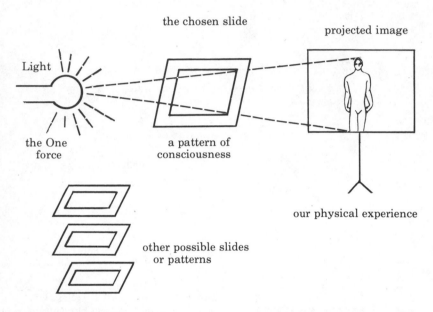

These principles can be illustrated by looking at just one of the centers or transducers. As an example, let us consider the third center, the adrenals. We are all familiar with the way in which this center is called into activity, even if we have not thought of it in just these terms. When it is operating in harmony with the whole system we may see something like persistence or courage; when it is out of harmony we are likely to see resentment, anger or fear. Such patterns of behavior (which are like the slides in our analogy) are stored at the various centers and are very real. They are the habit patterns or reactive tendencies that we have built. In discussing the qualities of consciousness related to the various centers, we have seen that certain types of habit patterns are especially related to particular centers. Depending on the mind's focus of attention, a particular slide or habit pattern from the storehouse of that center is put into a position where it is likely to be the one that will be projected onto the screen as our physical behavior. As the energy of the spirit moves through us and these patterns and gives us life, it manifests as our actions. If we have been dwelling upon angry or resentful thoughts, it is not surprising that we frequently end up behaving that way.

What we want to do in meditation is to develop a different way of responding. We want to have the activities of the centers acting together in a harmonious fashion. With our minds, we can remove the slide of resentful or angry patterns from its favored position and replace it with one that is more constructive. When we do this, we become truly different people. We begin to experience a kind of health that we have never known before. We begin to know a kind of joy and excitement in life that will give us a new sense of purposefulness. This is one thing that is taking place in meditation; by dwelling upon spiritually awakening affirmations, we are selecting new patterns—that is, patterns that are there already but usually do not get chosen. Then we are inviting the energy of the spirit to move through these spiritual centers to activate a creative, harmonious pattern for the body and the mind. This is one function of the spiritual center.

The other function is related to the phrase *opening a center*. Some people who refer to this process indicate that by following a certain meditation procedure they are able to open their spiritual centers. To open these centers means to modify the barrier between the infinite and the finite aspects of ourselves. Certainly, we are all seeking to lessen these barriers. However, how we go about doing so is of critical importance. The opening of the centers may be the normal accompaniment of deep meditation, or it may be brought about intentionally or accidentally by such stimuli as drugs, breathing exercises, certain yogic postures, mantras, incense, various religious rituals—for example, the dance of the whirling dervishes—or even physical disorders, such as spinal lesions.

The Center Works to Control the Flow of Energy

The more energy that is flowing through the transducer, the more intense will be the experience. As the center begins to open, more of the life force can begin to manifest through it into physical expression. Yet the intensity of an experience does not necessarily indicate the extent of spiritual growth. In fact, one possible explanation for the mind- and experience-altering properties of hallucinogenic drugs is that they have an effect on the spiritual centers, sometimes blowing them open. When some or all of the centers are opened, a significantly greater amount of energy is able to flow through, and very intense experiences are the result. The problem is that the patterns or slides within those centers are not changed by simply taking a drug. We may very well intensify the experience of patterns that will only take us even deeper into a sense of confusion.

In the interpretation of The Revelation which the readings offer, we find a clue as to the proper way to open the centers. It is suggested that the book with the seven seals represents the body with its seven centers. You will recall that John cries when he realizes that no one is worthy to open those seals. Then the Lamb appears (symbolic of the Christ), and it opens the seals. It is the spirit of the Christ that should open the spiritual centers of the body. Here we are being taught to meditate upon the Christ as an ideal and to invite Him into our lives. And then, as we work with expressing the qualities of Christ in the earth—as we live the life of love—these centers begin to open naturally. In this way, intense experiences come only as we are able to use them for our own growth. To optimize our own growth, it is better to allow the centers to open naturally through the action of the spirit as we work with meditation and apply what we know in daily life.

The Movement of Energy in Meditation

The spiritual centers serve as transducers throughout our daily activities. In meditation we seek to redirect the way in which the energy flows through these centers; as was mentioned earlier, our aim is to move the creative energy associated with the Leydig center directly to the pineal center. This movement, which in the East is referred to as the kundalini, is described in the following reading. It is apparent from this description that as the energy moves upward it takes its impulse from the adrenal center.

Q-1. Are the following statements true or false? Comment on each as I read it: The life force rises directly from the Leydig gland through the gonads, thence to pineal, and then to the other centers.
A-1. This is correct; though, to be sure, as it rises and is distributed through the other centers it returns to the solar plexus area for its impulse through the system.   281-53

In the following passage from the readings this kundalini pathway is referred to as the silver cord, which connects the cells of Leydig (or lyden) with the activities of the pineal and pituitary.

In the body we find that which connects the pineal, the pituitary, the lyden, may be truly called the silver cord, or the golden cup that may be filled with a closer walk with that which is the creative essence in physical, mental and spiritual life. . .   262-20

This awakening of energy during meditation takes place not only in the endocrine glands, but also throughout the entire nervous system. The following passage is in agreement with research into the physiology of meditation which indicates that the nervous system responds in a beneficial way during meditation.

Q-1. How can I overcome the nerve strain I'm under at times?
A-1. By closing the eyes and meditating from within, so that there arises—through that of the nerve system—that necessary element that makes along the *pineal* (don't forget that this runs from the toes to the crown of the head!), that will quiet the whole nerve forces, making for that—as has been given—as the *true* bread, the true strength of life itself. Quiet, meditation, for a half to a minute, will bring strength—will the body see *physically* this *flowing* out to quiet self, whether walking, standing still, or resting. Well, too, that *oft* when alone *meditate* in the silence—as the body *has done*.   311-4

This movement of energy throughout the body during meditation is experienced by different people in different ways. Some feel a slight pressure in the area of one of the spiritual centers, such as the heart region or the middle of the forehead. Some people feel tingling in certain parts of the body, such as the spine. Occasionally this experience is felt as two different energies, one moving upward from the base of the spine (the kundalini pathway), and the other, like the Pentecostal flames of the Holy Spirit, moving downward and touching the body in the region of the head. These two seemingly highly divergent experiences actually relate to the two poles within the body through which the one energy may flow.

As an illustration of the extremes of the ways in which the life force may flow between the two poles within, consider an automobile battery as an energy source. If a wrench is placed across the two poles, it will be melted by the direct flow of energy. If, on the other hand, the lead wires of an FM radio are placed on the two poles of the battery, the radio may pick up waves broadcast from a distant source and translate and amplify them into beautiful symphonic music. The energy is the same; the difference is in the complexity and order of the form—that is to say, the pattern—in which it flows. The selection of the pattern is very dependent upon the motives held in the imaginative force of the mind. There is within each of us a universal pattern—the law of love, the Christ pattern. This will be discussed in greater detail later, as we consider the role of an affirmation in meditation.

The Lord's Prayer

The readings suggest that the Lord's Prayer describes the proper movement of energy in meditation. This prayer can be used as a tool for the mind to ensure that this optimum condition is achieved. In the following passage from the readings we find the suggestion that the Lord's Prayer was given by Jesus specifically to relate to the opening of the spiritual centers.

Q-22. Does the outline of the Lord's Prayer as placed on our chart have any bearing on the opening of the centers?
A-22. Here is indicated the manner in which it was given as to the purpose for which it was given; not as an *only* way but as a way that would answer for those that sought to be—as others—seekers for *a* way, *an* understanding, to the relationships to the Creative Forces. It bears in relationships to this, then, the proper place.
Q-30. How should the Lord's Prayer be used in this connection?
A-30. As in feeling, as it were, the flow of the meanings of each portion of same throughout the body-physical. For as there is the response to the mental representations of all of these in the *mental* body, it may build into the physical body in the manner as He, thy Lord, thy Brother, so well expressed in, "I have bread ye know not of."   281-29

The second answer, in telling us how to use this prayer, suggests that as we focus our consciousness upon the prayer there is a response from a deep level of the mind ("the response to the mental representations of all of these in the *mental* body..."). This response from a deeper level of the mind is accompanied by a physiological response—there is an attunement that opens the flow of a more profound level of energy within us ("I have bread ye know not of"). This principle holds true whether we are focusing upon the Lord's Prayer or some other affirmation that contains our ideal for spiritual growth.

In the first answer above, a reference is made to a chart. In that chart the people asking the question had placed portions of the Lord's Prayer in relation to the various spiritual centers. The reading indicates that they had properly assigned these relationships. The chart looked much like this:

THE LORD'S PRAYER AND THE SEVEN CENTERS

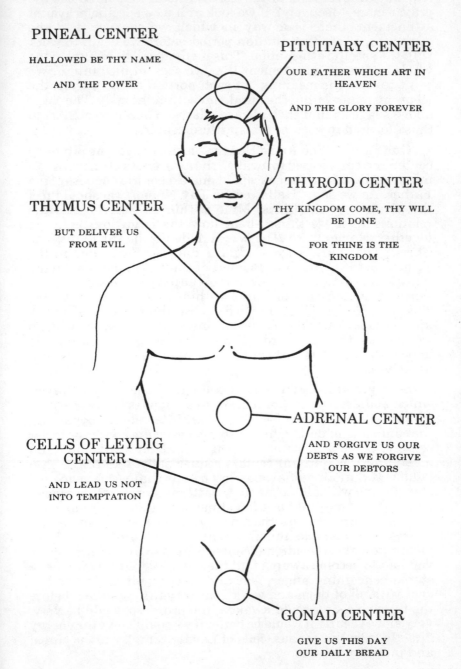

PINEAL CENTER

HALLOWED BE THY NAME

AND THE POWER

PITUITARY CENTER

OUR FATHER WHICH ART IN HEAVEN

AND THE GLORY FOREVER

THYROID CENTER

THY KINGDOM COME, THY WILL BE DONE

FOR THINE IS THE KINGDOM

THYMUS CENTER

BUT DELIVER US FROM EVIL

ADRENAL CENTER

AND FORGIVE US OUR DEBTS AS WE FORGIVE OUR DEBTORS

CELLS OF LEYDIG CENTER

AND LEAD US NOT INTO TEMPTATION

GONAD CENTER

GIVE US THIS DAY OUR DAILY BREAD

Can knowing this relationship between the spiritual centers and the various parts of the Lord's Prayer help us to use the prayer more effectively? If we look at it as a specific prayer of attunement, there is a way in which we can use it at the beginning of each meditation period before we begin to work with the specific affirmation. This method will be helpful in the whole process of attunement that we seek in meditation. We want to "feel the meaning" of each portion of the prayer, the meaning it has within the mind and within the body. The chart above suggests that each phrase relates to qualities similar to those focused in each of the spiritual centers.

"Our Father, Who Art in Heaven" is directed to the pituitary center and can be used to awaken the awareness of oneness. We might relate this to the concept of one God or the oneness of the Father. As we say, "Hallowed Be Thy Name," we should feel the presence of the Christ Mind within us. We can see this relationship if we think about how the following terms go together: Name, Word, The Word Made Flesh, The Light, The Christ. That part of the Godhead that is represented in the Trinity as the Christ has its point of contact in the body in the pineal center. As we say this part of the prayer, we want to get a sense of the presence of Christ within. "Thy Kingdom Come, Thy Will Be Done" is directed to the thyroid center and is appropriate to awaken a consciousness of the obedient will. So we can see that the Lord's Prayer begins by addressing the upper three centers, affirming the supremacy of God within ourselves.

We might think of the next section of the Lord's Prayer, which addresses the lower centers, as a "bypass" prayer. As the energy—the daily bread—rises, we are interested in bypassing the confusing or destructive patterns associated with the lower centers. Some schools of thought talk about awakening and mastering the spiritual centers sequentially, like rungs on a ladder. If that kind of awakening means that we have to deal step by step with all the memory patterns stored at these lower levels, then it may take us a long time to get the energy moved to the higher three centers. Such a way will be fraught with many snares. For example, imagine that you are sitting quietly in meditation and the adrenal center begins to awaken. Suppose you had to become aware of all the memory patterns you have stored concerning anger, fear and resentment. If you had to deal with all of them and work your way through them before the thymus center could awaken, the progress would be very, very slow. Clearly it would be better if we could move the energy directly from the gonads/cells of Leydig complex to the pineal and pituitary centers.

This is *not* to suggest that we are not responsible for the things that we have built into the spiritual centers in between. Certainly we are responsible for those patterns. But the question is, How do we want to work on healing? Do we want to fight our negative patterns at their own level (and be there a long time), or do we want to move to a higher level of awareness and energy and from that level begin to deal with them through the power of the Spirit of Christ? Patterns related to the earth must invariably win if they are fought at their own level. But we have the alternative of awakening this spiritual energy to which we have greater access in meditation and letting it move directly to the higher centers. There it will take on a vibrational quality that is in accord with the Christ and the principle of oneness. Then the energy can move back down and heal the patterns of the lower centers. This is referred to by some Chinese schools of meditation as the circulation of the light. The truth of these concepts will become experienced by all of us as we continue to work with meditation.

As we are sitting still, dwelling upon an affirmation, it is likely that some memory will be awakened. An image or thought will come to mind, or our thoughts may simply drift off. What could be happening is that a memory pattern associated with one of the lower centers is asking for attention. What do we want to do at that moment? Dwell on the thought? Try to solve the problem at its own level? Or do we want to let go of it, move to a higher perspective and have it healed? If we choose the latter alternative, energy flows back down and cleanses the lower centers. As this happens we may not realize what patterns are being healed, but undoubtedly we will see changes in our daily life confirming this healing.

And so the Lord's Prayer begins by addressing the higher centers and then speaks to the lower centers. In essence, the message directed to the lower centers is: As the energy awakens, let it move through each of you without awakening patterns that are out of harmony with the ideal. First the Prayer addresses the gonads, which have been described as a motor or generator of the body. It says, "Give Us This Day Our Daily Bread"; thus, with this phrase we are requesting access in this meditation (or this day) to only that amount of energy that we can use constructively—no more than that. We might remember the story of the Israelites in the desert and the way in which they received their daily food, manna. Each morning they were to collect only the amount that was needed for that day—any excess would spoil on them. In the Lord's Prayer we are seeking that there may be awakened only that energy which is needed now to do the things we need to do.

Next the prayer addresses the solar plexus or adrenal centers:

"Forgive Us Our Debts as We Forgive Our Debtors." Here we want to focus on the quality of forgiveness. When we can do this, the energy is able to move on and not get caught up in the awakening of old patterns of fear or resentment. Certainly we may have problems at the level of this spiritual center, but we are going to deal with them later, as the energy flows down.

Then the prayer moves on and addresses the cells of Leydig with the words, "Lead Us Not into Temptation." That is to say, "Do not allow the energy to dwell here and awaken the patterns at this level." The constant temptation is to look at life in terms of duality instead of oneness—to think of God as being apart from us. The cells of Leydig center has especially to do with this sense of division, which is reflected in the male-female polarity. As we bring an ideal into our work of balancing the male and female energies within us, we experience underlying oneness. So here we can focus on and feel that presence within, which leads us and directs us.

And finally, the prayer addresses the thymus center, saying, "Deliver Us from Evil." Again, the idea expressed here is "Do not allow the energy to awaken the patterns at this level." If we think of evil as the lack of love, then we can see the relationship between these words and the thymus center. We are speaking to the center and asking that the energy pass through and not awaken patterns associated with memories of our failure to love truly.

The prayer ends by affirming again the Triune Godhead within: "For Thine Is the Kingdom, the Power and the Glory Forever." In saying this prayer and feeling its meaning we are moving toward the optimum physical conditions for meditation.

Chapter Four

MEDITATION

Definitions of Meditation

The Edgar Cayce readings offer several definitions of meditation. In each case, the focus is upon an attunement process which involves the aligning or harmonizing of the body, mind, and soul of man. Such an attunement makes it possible for man to attune the spirit within to the Universal Spirit.

What *is* meditation?
It is not musing, not daydreaming; but as ye find your bodies made up of the physical, mental and spiritual, it is the attuning of the mental body and the physical body to its spiritual source.
281-41

Meditation **is *emptying* self of all that hinders the creative forces from rising along the natural channels of the physical man to be disseminated through those centers and sources that create the activities of the physical, the mental, the spiritual man; properly done must make one *stronger* mentally, physically . . .**
281-13

There are certain concepts expressed in these definitions that should be emphasized. First is the word "natural." Meditation is not to be understood as an attempt by man to create physical, mental or spiritual experiences that he is not meant to have. The creative energies within man seek to flow upward and lift his consciousness. The drive to raise one's consciousness is just as natural, or indeed more natural, than the physical drives of the body such as hunger, thirst, and sex.

Don't seek for unnatural or supernatural! It is the natural— it is nature—it is God's activity! His associations with man— His *desire* to make for man a way for an understanding!
5754-3

A second significant concept in these definitions is that there exists that which can hinder or block man's contact with the spiritual source. The process of meditation relates directly to how one can deal with those hindrances. We might think of such hindrances as the accumulation of thought forms, desire patterns and their accompanying physical processes. These limiting and selfish patterns are built throughout the history of the soul. Meditation is *"emptying* self of all that hinders," or letting go of our involvement with those patterns that would limit us, in favor of a higher pattern that will restore the awareness of our true nature. The readings indicate that these same thought patterns which create an obstacle in meditation are involved in the process of the attraction of the soul back into the earth time and again. As we deal with these patterns in meditation, we are beginning to free ourselves from the cycle of incarnations. A definition of meditation from *The Secret of the Golden Flower* emphasizes this point:

> The circulation of the light is not only the circulation
> of the seed-blossom of the individual body, but it is even
> the circulation of the true, creative, formative energies.
> It is not a momentary fantasy, but the exhaustion of the
> cycle (of soul migrations) of all the aeons.   p. 32

Perhaps the most concise yet comprehensive definition is that meditation is the practicing of the first part of the great commandment:

> Thou shalt love the Lord thy God with all thy heart,
> and with all thy soul, and with all thy mind.
> Matthew 22:37

Reflection upon this great commandment should give us some insight into the true spirit and purpose of meditation.

The Purpose of Meditation

Understood properly, the true purpose for practicing meditation should be the desire to be one with God because of our love for Him. We must be careful that we do not make a mental list of reasons for meditating, such as "I am going to meditate because it will make me more healthy, more psychic, and more able to get by on less sleep." When we do this our motivation is to get something for ourselves. If we wish to move away from the language of karma and conditionality, and into the language of love, we must be eager to meditate simply because we seek to be attuned to God. To do otherwise—to set expectations or seek results—would be like a man saying to his wife, "I am going to love you so that I will be sure that you will do these certain things for me." The readings express this point by warning us not to "meditate for" but to "meditate to." Our concern should not be for the results that may come from regular meditation; rather, our aim should be to grow to a state of attunement with the spiritual source. In a reading recommending that he begin a program of regular meditation, one man was told:

This we would keep, but don't be anxious about it. Let it be a necessity to thy better being, rather than giving or having the meditation for better being. It's like whether you are baptized for or baptized to! It's the same application within the inner self. You have the meditation because you desire to be attuned with Creative Forces. You don't have the meditation because it's a duty or because you want to feel better, but to attune self to the Infinite! . . .   **1861-18**

The Easter tradition stresses much the same approach as is recommended in the reading above; this approach is illustrated in the following story. A man once came to the Buddha to discuss his long practice of meditation. He said, "I have been meditating for twenty years, and now I can levitate across the river." The Buddha replied, "You have been wasting your time. For a nickel you could have taken the boat at any time."

There are many benefits which may accrue from the regular practice of meditation, including psychic development and miraculous or magical powers, or *siddhis,* as they are called in the East. However, our love for and desire to be one with God should be the motivating purpose and spirit of meditation. Of course that desire finds its manifestation in our compliance with the second part of the commandment (to love our neighbor as ourselves) as we, in our daily lives, apply and become that spirit of love which we have awakened in our meditation. Nevertheless, we must not concern ourselves with results. The *Bhagavad-Gita* says,

He who does the task dictated by duty, caring nothing for the fruit of the action, he is a yogi, a true sannyasin.
                                                                            p. 62

In *The Secret of the Golden Flower* we read,

The decision must be carried out with a collected heart, and not seeking success; success will then come of itself.   p. 40

The Bible expresses the same thought in these words:

God giveth the increase.   I Corinthians 2:7

And the readings say,

. . . don't be anxious about it.   **1861-18**

Another story from the East tells of a chela who came to his guru and said, "Master, I want to see God!" Immediately the teacher grasped his student by the hair, dragged him into the nearby river, and held his head under water while he struggled, nearly drowning. Then the guru raised him up and calmly said, "When you want to see God as much as you wanted that breath of air, you may begin to make some progress."

Reading the Song of Solomon in the Old Testament can give us a sense of the longing of the lover for the loved one. We must then transfer that awareness quickly to awaken a deeper feeling for the great commandment to love God with all our hearts and minds and souls.

The second side of the motivational basis for meditation—which corresponds to the second portion of the commandment, to love our neighbor as ourselves—can be amplified by reflecting on this passage from *The Secret of the Golden Flower:*

> One must not content oneself with small demands but must rise to the thought that all living creatures have to be redeemed. One must not be trivial and irresponsible in heart, but must strive to make deeds prove one's words.   p. 48

The purpose of meditation, combined with application, is to *live* the great commandment, "to love God with all your heart...and your neighbor as yourself." (Matthew 22: 37, 39)

Preparation for Meditation

In meditation we are dealing with a great power; preparation is most prudent. As Jesus admonished His disciples, we should not approach the temple without putting things right with our fellow man.

> Therefore if thou bring thy gift to the altar, and there rememberest that thy brother hath aught against thee; leave there thy gift before the altar, and go thy way; first be reconciled to thy brother, and then come and offer thy gift.   Matthew 5:23-24

One continuously applicable implication of this teaching is that if we intend to approach the throne daily in our meditation, we must also be about correcting things in our daily lives. Such preparation is an individual matter. The Old Testament preparations for the tabernacle worship are very challenging in this regard. Each person must decide for himself what activities create a greater sense of devotion and openness for meditation. Some find that cleansing the physical body is important. Others find particular exercises or disciplines helpful. Many feel that a prayer of protection at the beginning of meditation is important. One such prayer is:

> Father, as I open myself to the unseen forces that surround the throne of grace and beauty and might, I throw about myself the protection found in the thought of the Christ.

One shouldn't just utter this as a magic ritual and then expect that he is going to be protected. Instead, one should use it as an aid for sensing or experiencing the true protective presence of the Christ.

Certainly, for every person, attitudes and emotions are a significant aspect of preparation. The way that we have been using the mind in our daily lives will have a great effect upon our capacity to still and focus it in meditation. Thus, preparation is not just the things that we do five or ten minutes before the meditation period. We are constantly preparing ourselves.

For the promise has ever been, look *within!* Meet thy Maker in the temple within. For the body is indeed the temple of the living God, and He has promised to meet thee there, in the holy of holies, in the mount within. And His promises are sure.

How has been the pattern in such meetings? Has not the edict been ever, "Purify yourselves, your bodies, for on the morrow *thy God* would speak with thee"?

Hast thou not learned, He is ever the same, yesterday, today, and forever?

Then prepare thyself in that way and manner that seemeth to *thee,* in *thine* experience, in thy consciousness to meet thy Maker.

Then as ye use those material preparations, they only give to the body a greater consciousness—through their application to the body—of the necessity of every atom cooperating in that direction!   1152-2

Q-2. Just what preparation would you advise for the body, now?

A-2. This should be rather the choice of the body from its *own* development, than from what *any* other individual entity or source might give.

Purify the body, purify the mind; that the principle, the choice of ideals as made by the entity may be made manifest.

Do whatever is required for this—whether the washing of the body, the surrounding with this or that influence, or that of whatever nature.   2475-1

The Use of an Affirmation

The basic principle in the readings concerning the practice of meditation is that the spirit and purpose are more important than technique. We should each begin with the best understanding that we have of how to meet God within the temple, which is the body. Yes, we must learn to meditate, but growth in understanding and attunement can always take place from whatever point at which we find ourselves. We must be assured in the depths of our being that it is not we ourselves, the meditators, that do the work, but the power of the spirit within, which is responsive to our sincerity and openness. We must neither place limitation on the way in which the spirit can work nor expect to manipulate that spirit by adherence to proper ritual. The question always arises in the mind of the meditator as to whether or not he is using the proper technique. When one person asked if she were meditating properly, the readings replied, "Be confident that in Him all things are done well." This answer may be more instructive than it seems at first glance. The sense that *He is meditating me* should alleviate all doubts about proper procedure. It is the process of being moved by the intensity of the desire and then letting go, of "effortless effort," that allows the infinite forces to begin to interpenetrate and transform the finite man.

As we come to understand that the body is the temple and that the Old Testament instructions for the tabernacle worship are externally projected patterns of internal processes, we come to the principle that all external rituals of worship may be projections of the patterns of attunement processes. For example, the sacrifice of the best animals in the flock symbolizes a willingness to give up our favorite lower emotions in preference for attunement. The study of the symbology of the Mass should be highly instructive regarding the inner process of attunement in meditation.

On occasion it becomes the hope of practitioners of religious rituals that if they but perform the ritual properly, regardless of their motive and spirit, they can be assured of the efficacious flow of the power of God. This way of thinking can also become a problem for the meditator, who may hope for results due to proper (even scientific) technique, with no consideration of either motive or application.

Are there procedures which enhance the meditation experience? To be sure, and these will be given in step-by-step detail; however, they are guides to, not guarantees of, attunement.

Who shall ascend into the hill of the Lord? or who shall stand in his holy place? He that hath clean hands, and a pure heart . . .   Psalm 24:3-4

Some of the readings indicate that the use of certain aids or techniques should be adopted as the *result* of attunement, not as the *cause*. If we become too focused upon the form or the technique of these procedures, it is easy to lose sight of the true sense of the purpose of meditation.

When you are moved by full accord, use the intonations, the breathing, the posture; but let this be rather an outgrowth of attunement than the purpose *for* attunement.   281-35

If *form* becomes that that is the guiding element, then the hope or the faith is lost in form!   262-17

We must not wait until we think we have the right technique to begin to meditate. No technique will ensure His presence—only a sincere and open invitation will.

Among the ideas suggested in the readings on meditation are the effectiveness of working with a small group, the desirability of choosing the same place and time each day, and the importance of keeping the spine straight, performing breathing exercises, chanting, and using incense properly. Concern over the amount of time that we should spend in daily meditation can cause us to lose sight of the purpose of meditating. The effects of just a moment of contact with the inner self far outweigh those of sitting for hours without the proper attitude or motivation, trying to meditate.

How long was the experience of Saul in the way to Damascus? How long was the experience of Stephen as he saw the Master standing—not sitting, *standing?* How long was the experience of those that saw the vision that beckoned to them, or any such experience? . . .

For, did the Father (or Infinity) bring the earth, the worlds into existence, how much greater is a day in the house of the Lord—or a moment in His presence—than a thousand years in carnal forces?

Hence a soul even for a flash, or for a breath, has perhaps experienced even as much as Saul in the way.   262-57

Spend that time necessary to know you are in accord, but spend more time in carrying out the directions given in such periods. For unless one may make practical in daily life the tenets or teachings [obtained by meditation], these are worth little to the entity itself.   3513-1

Undoubtedly, the most important suggestion from the readings concerns what to do with the mind during meditation. That which is held mentally in meditation is that which is being built. As a tool for the attunement process of meditation, the readings recommend the use of an affirmation—a brief statement of the ideal or purpose towards which the meditator seeks to grow.

Whereas some schools of meditation see the mind as the enemy and would teach that it must be blanked out for proper meditation to occur, the approach described in the readings is based upon the principle that "the mind is the way." This is not to deny that the mind includes habits and memories that are stumbling blocks in meditation. However, it does suggest that meditation must be a holistic process. The mind plays the vital role in attuning both the physical and the mental to the spiritual source. Also, the readings suggest that written on the mind as a pattern is the awareness of our oneness with God, which we seek to awaken.

Our understanding of the role of the mind in meditation is closely tied to the distinction between prayer and meditation. Prayer is an activity of the conscious mind. It is an outpouring of conscious thoughts in our attempt to attune ourselves to God. On the other hand, meditation involves a quieting of the conscious mind; it is a receptive state. To use a simple analogy, prayer would be talking to God, and meditation would be listening. Both of these practices are important to our spiritual growth. Our capacity to meditate effectively is closely related to our ability to pray effectively.

The Edgar Cayce readings (and some other sources) describe the use of the mind in meditation as being twofold. First, we seek to awaken with the imaginative forces a particular response in the mental body. Then, having awakened that consciousness, we seek to be still, quiet and receptive. This "alert listening" stance of the mind allows the awakened pattern of this higher state of consciousness literally to be built into our physical bodies.

To look more closely at the purpose and practice of using an affirmation, consider the following reading. Keep in mind that the affirmation should be a capsulization of that which we have chosen as our spiritual ideal.

Q-1. How may I bring into activity my pineal and pituitary glands, as well as the kundalini and other chakras, that I may attain to higher mental and spiritual powers. Are there exercises for this purpose . . . ?
A-1. . . . first so *fill* the mind with the ideal that it may vibrate throughout the whole of the *mental* being!

Then, close the desires of the fleshly self to conditions about same. Meditate upon *"Thy will with me."* Feel same. Fill *all* the centers of the body, from the lowest to the highest, with that ideal; opening the centers by surrounding self first with that consciousness, "Not my will but Thine, O Lord, be done in and through me."   1861-4

In this passage, two affirmations are suggested—one an abbreviated version of the other. However, in each case the ideal expressed involves the meditator's desire to make his will one with the divine will. The reading first suggests that the spirit of this state of mind be allowed to fill the entire mental being. This of course involves a one-pointedness of mind. The reading then goes on to suggest that as this is done there will be a response within the body that perhaps may even be felt. That response will be especially related to the activities of the seven spiritual centers. Some have found that at the beginning of meditation it is helpful actually to think of those seven spiritual centers and to visualize them being filled with light or with the consciousness of the ideal. However, it is not necessary, nor even advisable, to think about the spiritual centers throughout the meditation period. As we are able to sustain a one-pointedness of mind and purpose, the appropriate physiological response will take place naturally.

A question frequently arises as to whether or not achieving the beneficial results of meditation is simply a matter of saying the words of the affirmation. Certainly there is a long tradition according to which power is associated with particular words. It is possible that the major reason for the commandment regarding taking the Lord's name in vain was to retain the energy-evoking qualities of the names of God and their potential for aiding us in attuning to His presence within. However, many sources suggest that drawing upon this power is not simply a matter of saying the word. The verbal sound must be accompanied by an inner awareness of the word's deepest spiritual meaning. The most immediate application of this principle to our practice of meditation lies in the fact that the affirmation is not to be repeated over and over again. As the Master said, " . . . use not vain repetitions . . . " (Matthew 6:7) Instead, we should feel the meaning behind the words, and this requires periods of silence.

It also should be noted that we are not to do an intellectual analysis of the affirmation during meditation. On the contrary, we should focus our attention on awakening the spirit within the words. Intellectual analysis of the affirmation has its place, but it should be done before the actual meditation period.

A word from Eastern traditions of meditation which relates

closely to our concept of an affirmation is *mantra*. The definition of a mantra as a mind tool is explained in the following passage.

In the word "mantra" the root "man" equals "to think" (in Greek, "menos," Latin "mens") is combined with the element "tra," which forms tool-words. Thus "mantra" is a "tool for thinking" . . .
(*Foundations of Tibetan Mysticism,* p. 19)

The emphasis here should be upon the concept that a mantra (or an affirmation) is a *tool* that the mind can utilize to become attuned to the spirit. We bring the mind to stillness by *using* the mind, not by denying its place or existence. Through the activity of the mind, with the aid of a tool such as a mantra or an affirmation, the mind is brought into alignment with the spirit. Yet there is nothing magical about mantras or affirmations in themselves. For this reason, we might do well to discard the noun mantra in preference for the adverb mantrically. To use an affirmation mantrically means to quicken the inner essence or spirit behind the words with the imaginative forces, and to allow that spirit so to fill the mind as to awaken a transformative response within the physical body. It is, of course, important to remember that this transformative work of meditation is done by the spirit within and that the affirmation serves only to direct or focus upon these spiritual forces.

Mantras do not act on account of their own "magic" nature, but only through the mind that experiences them. They do not possess any power of their own; they are only the means for concentrating already existing forces—just as a magnifying glass, though it does not contain any heat of its own, is able to concentrate the rays of the sun and to transform their mild warmth into incandescent heat.
(*Foundations of Tibetan Mysticism,* pp. 27-28)

The function of affirmations that is suggested in the Edgar Cayce readings might be better understood by considering another Eastern term, *dharanis.*

Dharanis are means for fixing the mind upon an idea, a vision or an experience gained in meditation. They may represent the quintessence of a teaching as well as the experience of a certain state of consciousness, which hereby can be recalled or recreated deliberately at any time. Therefore they are also called supporters, receptacles or bearers of wisdom (vidyadhara). They are not different from mantras in their function but to some extent in their form, in so far as they may attain a considerable length and sometimes represent a combination of many mantras or "seed-syllables" (bija-mantras), or the quintessence of a sacred text. They were a product as well as a means of meditation: "Through deep absorption (samadhi) one gains a truth, through a dharani one fixes and retains it."

(*Foundations of Tibetan Mysticism*, pp. 31-32)

Let us consider the affirmations given for the Search for God Study Group to be, by this definition, dharanis. Thus, these affirmations "are not different from mantras in their function but to some extent in their form, in so far as they may attain a considerable length and sometimes represent a combination of many mantras or 'seed-syllables.'" The Search for God readings may be thought of as "a sacred text" of which the affirmations represent "the quintessence." They were "a product" (of Edgar Cayce's meditation, or samadhi) as well as "a means of meditation" for us, to be used as "supporters, receptacles or bearers of wisdom."

In the light of these suggestions, let us consider the wisdom of the approach put forth in *A Search for God*. The particular chapter under consideration constitutes the "sacred text," which gives us a new understanding of spiritual law. With the affirmation, as "the quintessence" of that text, we awaken an authentic spirit within ourselves. Then with the selection of a discipline (or an experiment) we apply that truth and truly "fix and retain it." Thus we have a *triple* "method of making fast the enlightenment," in place of the double method mentioned below.

Now let us inquire one step deeper into the use of the affirmation in relationship to the *silence*. In *The Secret of the Golden Flower* we find some especially helpful, though difficult, instructions:

Fixating contemplation is indispensable; it insures the making fast of the enlightenment. Only one must not stay sitting rigidly if worldly thoughts come up, but one must examine where the thought is, where it began, and where it fades out . . . When the flight of thoughts keep extending further, one should stop and begin contemplating. Let one contemplate and then start fixating again. That is the double method of making fast the enlightenment. It means the circulation of the light.   p. 36

Several of the words and phrases used here might be translated into expressions used in the readings. The word "fixation" refers to being silent while the integrative hormonal secretions move to every cell in the body. This is literally "circulation." "Contemplation" can be understood as the awakening of the response through focusing attention upon an affirmation. Finally, "light" is one Creative Force allowed to flow by the awakening motive. If we use these definitions along with some additional rewording, the above passage might read:

Being silent after awakening the response is indispensable. It ensures that the effect of the good spirit that is awakened will be felt in the tissues and cells of the body ... When the flight of thoughts keeps extending further, one should stop and return to awaken the spirit with the affirmation. Let one affirm and then be silent again. That is the double method of making fast the enlightenment.

The text continues by offering a pair of equivalencies. This is followed by a description of the two fundamental problems that can arise for the meditator.

The circulation is fixation. The light is contemplation. Fixation without contemplation is circulation without light. Contemplation without fixation is light without circulation. Take note of that!
p. 36

"The circulation is fixation!" As soon as the one energy begins to move in meditation, it is building *something*. Any time we are dealing with the one energy, the mind is patterning and crystalizing it (at the fourth-dimensional level). "The light is contemplation." Within an affirmation, such as the Lord's Prayer, there is an expression of the Christ pattern, the Light. If we will use the affirmation correctly—that is, with openness and sincerity of purpose—we will have access to that perfect pattern written within ourselves from the beginning. (See p. 9, chapter one, which discusses this pattern.)

As an interpretation of the remainder of the quoted passage, consider two hypothetical meditators—A and B—each of whom makes one of the two fundamental mistakes in the practice of meditation. A is able to concentrate in meditation, dwell upon a mantric thought, and sense the movement of energy through himself. Yet, he has focused his mind upon something less than an expression of the highest ideal that he

58

knows. Let us suppose that he has chosen to focus his attention on sex. "Fixation without contemplation is circulation without light." Without a spiritual intent and purpose held in mind, the movement and patterning of energy fails to fulfill the transformative potential of the meditative process.

B has chosen to use an affirmation which expresses the highest ideal that she knows, yet in her attempt to meditate she is unable to go beyond just repeating it over and over. The stillness of resting in the spirit of the affirmation is essential. "Contemplation without fixation is light without circulation." For the full potential of meditation to be realized, the strictly intellectual part of the mind must let go and allow the flow and fixation of the pattern of love expressed in the affirmation.

How are we to use the silence? We should awaken a motivational response and hold that feeling in the silence. If we drift away we can, as *The Secret of the Golden Flower* says, "make a medicine of the illness." We do this by taking just enough note of the distracting thought to renew a sense that only the Spirit of Christ can handle that concern. We are remotivated to attune ourselves to Him; we return to the spirit of the affirmation and hold the silence again.

We can now combine these insights from the Edgar Cayce readings and from several Eastern texts to produce a comprehensive and systematic approach to the use of affirmations. Our approach will be based upon the following three important principles:

(1) The term *mind* can refer to more than just the intellectual, analytical function of mind. There exists as well the intuitive, feeling and imaginative faculties of the mind.

(2) There is already written upon the mind (the soul-mind) of every individual the pattern of the awareness of our oneness with God. It is this pattern within the mind that we seek to awaken during meditation.

(3) Until we become extremely adept in deep meditation, our meditation periods will tend to move back and forth between two poles. On the one hand, there is the conscious effort through prayer or the words of an affirmation to awaken in the conscious mind a particular state of awareness. On the other hand, once that awareness has been awakened, we hold the essence of its spirit in *silence*. It is only when we have lost the feeling or the spirit associated with the affirmation that we move back to say and feel the words again.

In principle, this systematic approach may seem very simple. However, in practice it may take years of work before we are able to hold in silence for prolonged periods the spirit of our affirmation. Let us consider some of the problems that may arise. Imagine that you have been sitting in silence, with your attention held one-pointedly upon the spirit of your ideal, but after a time you realize that your mind has wandered off. Perhaps you hear an airplane passing overhead; perhaps you hear a child playing out in the street, and you catch yourself following that distraction. At this point there are several things that you can do.

One is to become very upset with yourself, to become very discouraged or frustrated and say, "Oh, I'm never going to learn how to do this." However, this reaction is contrary to the spirit you are trying to awaken in meditation, and it is actually counterproductive. Such thoughts of self-criticism will not be helpful when your mind wanders from the affirmation.

Another possibility is simply to bring yourself back to your one-pointed focus by saying your affirmation again. This method will often be effective; however, it involves one serious difficulty. Recall that in meditation we are seeking to awaken the consciousness of oneness and wholeness. If we start trying to block out external or internal distractions, we have created a sense of duality: on the one hand, there are those things that we think of as being helpful to our meditation; on the other, there are those that we try to block out because we feel they are detrimental.

Although such a process of forced concentration may be somewhat successful, there is a third alternative. This involves using the distraction to take you deeper into meditation. It is a matter of letting a stumbling block become a stepping-stone, using a weakness and making it into a strength, or making "a medicine of the illness."

Let us consider two simple examples of experiences you might have. Imagine yourself sitting in meditation, using the affirmation "Let me be a channel of blessings to others." For a time you are able to focus on feeling the inner meaning of these words. You are maintaining the silence, only occasionally finding it necessary to repeat the words. Then a plane passes overhead and you catch yourself thinking about the plane. Once again, you have several alternatives: you can get frustrated with yourself or with the pilot of the plane; you can just say the affirmation again, yanking your attention back and seeking to block out this distraction; or you can choose the third alternative and seek to use the distraction to take you deeper into meditation. In this case doing this would involve taking a moment to be a channel of blessings to the people in that plane, saying a brief prayer for them. This may take ten or fifteen seconds, but at some point you will find yourself back in the spirit of the words of the affirmation.

Now imagine a second example, one in which you are using

the same affirmation and an internal distraction arises. Suppose you find yourself thinking about some difficult, troublesome situation at work. Instead of becoming frustrated with your mind for having wandered off, and instead of trying to block out this thought, you might make use of the distraction by taking a moment to be a channel of blessings to this situation at work. Through a few moments of prayer directed toward this condition, you will once again find yourself back in the spirit of your affirmation, feeling the inner meaning of its words. The diagram below is a simple illustration of this process.

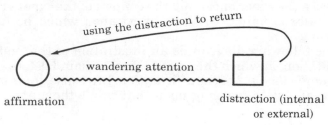

The following diagram is an adaptation of a model developed earlier in this book. Recall that our initial model involved three primary levels of mind: conscious, subconscious and superconscious. In this adaptation we are using planes instead of sections of a cone to represent these three levels. In the diagram below we also find a symbolic representation of the use of an affirmation in meditation. The letter P in the superconscious region symbolizes the highest pattern of wholeness and oneness, which already exists within us (i.e., the Christ Consciousness). The letter W at the right of our model symbolizes the words of our affirmation, an affirmation which capsulizes our spiritual ideal. The letter A represents the conscious awareness that those words are potentially able to awaken within us. Our purpose in meditation is to awaken a consciousness which has some correspondence with that perfect pattern within the superconscious mind.

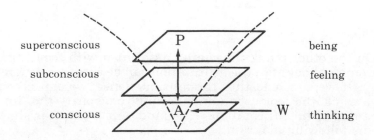

Now let us consider the qualities of these three planes of experience. *Thinking* is especially characteristic of the conscious mind. *Feeling* (in the sense of emotions) is a function of the subconscious mind; in dealing with this level it is important to note that there are feelings or emotions related to the upper three spiritual centers. Finally, the experience of *beingness* itself relates to the superconscious mind.

In the first two functions—thinking and feeling—we have aspects of duality. There is the experiencer, and there is that which he can observe as the content of experience—whether it is a thought or a feeling. At the third level there is a oneness between the experiencer and the content of the experience—the meditator is united with the spirit upon which he has been focusing.

The following diagram is an illustration of the first step of meditation, in which the entire conscious mind is focused upon the *single thought* of the affirmation. In a sense, there is energy associated with focusing upon that single thought.

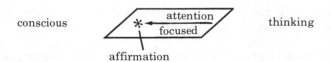

What frequently happens is that quite soon the mind begins to wander around, being distracted by other thoughts. Periodically, we become aware of what we are doing and direct the mind back to the affirmation. But during meditation periods in which this happens continually, our focus remains primarily at the thinking level. This activity might accurately be characterized as a reverie or a daydream. It is illustrated in the diagram below.

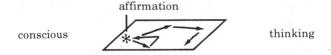

On the other hand, the energy associated with focusing on the single thought of the affirmation can be used in a different way. If we can hold that thought in silence, we can become aware of the corresponding feeling or spirit—the inner meaning of the affirmation. This kind of movement is shown in the following diagram.

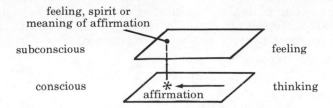

However, even focusing upon the feeling of the affirmation involves a concentration of energy. Many people find that after a few moments that energy is used to drift to a different feeling. Once we have arrived at a different feeling, it will usually awaken a corresponding thought at the thinking level. The thought will of course be perceived as a distracting one. This process happens very quickly; one moment we are silently holding the feeling of our affirmation, and the next thing we know we are thinking about something totally unrelated to our purpose in meditation. However, if we go back and examine what has taken place, we will likely find that just before the distracting thought came to mind we had drifted into the associated feeling. This process is illustrated below.

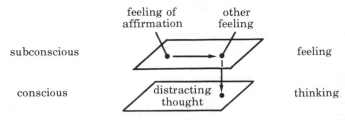

Once we have moved back down to the thought level, we must once again focus the imaginative forces upon the single thought of the affirmation. The diagram immediately above demonstrates one of the key points in our work with an affirmation. What we must learn to do is to catch ourselves at the feeling level and return immediately to the feeling associated with the affirmation. What are the feelings to which we drift away? Many people have found that they wander into feelings of doubt and fear (e.g., the fear of going any deeper into meditation) or into the feelings about daily life which they were entertaining just before meditation.

If we can hold in silence that single feeling, then the energy associated with focusing at that point can be used to move once again—this time to the level of *being*. Here we are one with the ideal that is expressed by the affirmation. Here we are that ideal. There is a transformation in consciousness and we experience our oneness with God. This is the aim of deep meditation—to experience this kind of unity. It is not enough just to hold the thought of the affirmation, nor is it enough just to feel it; we must become one with its essence.

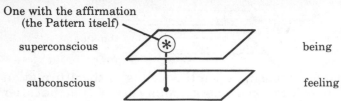

One with the affirmation (the Pattern itself)

superconscious   being

subconscious   feeling

In *Mysticism* (1910), by Evelyn Underhill, we find a close parallel to this concept of three levels of experience in attunement. Underhill describes three stages of meditative experience, which are summarized below. Especially important to note is her warning that we must not think of meditation as stopping at the first or the second stage.

1. "Recollection," the first stage, is the most difficult, because it involves going against the habits and impulses of the mind, which requires a determined act of will. An individual may spend years in this first stage.

> All the scattered interests of the self have here to be collected; there must be a deliberate and unnatural act of attention, a deliberate expelling of all discordant images from the consciousness—a hard and ungrateful task. Since the transcendental faculties are still young and weak, the senses not wholly mortified, it needs a stern determination, a willful choice, if we are to succeed in concentrating our attention upon the whispered message from within, undistracted by the loud voices which besiege us from without.   p. 313

2. The second stage is the experience of "Quiet." It is a level of experience "for which human speech has few equivalents . . . and which is characterized by an immense increase in the receptivity of the self, and an almost complete suspension of the reflective powers." (p. 317) In this stage the struggle to concentrate is gone and a "self-acting recollection" is present. Many initially experience this stage as startling because of the deprivation of all accustomed mental workings.

The Quiet stage is potentially the most misleading to the spiritual seeker. The alert stillness of this state can turn to the limp passivity that has characterized Quietism. The adherents of this movement have mistaken the peace and regeneration of this state to be the goal. Mystics who have understood that the

Quiet is *not* an end in itself have also been subjected to accusations that have been directed at the Quietists.

> "Quiet" is the danger-zone of introversion. Of all forms of mystical activity, perhaps this has been the most abused, the least understood. Its theory, seized upon, divorced from its context, and developed to excess, produced the foolish and dangerous exaggerations of Quietism: and these, in their turn, caused a wholesale condemnation of the principle of passivity, and make many superficial persons regard "naked orison" as an essentially heretical act. The accusation of Quietism has been hurled at mystics whose only fault was a looseness of language which laid them open to misapprehension.   p. 322

Underhill describes Quietism as "absorption in nothing at all," with the purpose to "luxuriate in its peaceful effects." (p. 324) She mentions the transcendentalists as examples of this movement, which suggests the possible conclusion that Transcendental Meditation (as currently taught in this country, but introduced long after Underhill's book was published) leads most of its followers into the temptation and potential entrapment of this second stage.

> Much of the teaching of modern "mystical" cults is thus crudely quietistic. It insists on the necessity of "going into the silence," and even, with a strange temerity, gives preparatory lessons in subconscious meditation: a procedure which might well provoke the laughter of the saints. The faithful, being gathered together, are taught by simple exercises in recollection the way to attain the "Quiet." By this mental trick the modern transcendentalist naturally attains to a state of vacant placidity, in which he rests: and "remaining in a distracted idleness and misspending the time in expectation of extraordinary visits," believes—with a faith which many of the orthodoxy might envy—that he is here "united with his Principle."   p. 324

In contrast to this is the understanding that the Quiet is a stage of *preparation*. It is only an opening of the door, and "that which comes in when the door is opened will be that which we truly and passionately desire." (p. 324)

3. In the third stage, which is called "Contemplation," the self transcends the stillness of Quiet and is "energized enthusiastically on those high levels which are dark to the

intellect but radiant to the heart." (p. 328) The greatest contemplatives have been able to sustain this third state for only the briefest of moments. Underhill defines two conditions that are present in this experience.

Whatever terms he may employ to describe it, and however faint or confused his perceptions may be, the mystic's experience in Contemplation is the experience of the All, and this experience seems to be *given* rather than attained.

This revealed reality is apprehended by way of participation, not by way of observation. The passive receptivity of the Quiet is here developed into an active, outgoing self-donation, which is the self's response to the Divine initiative.   p. 333

Experiences in Meditation

There are two types of experiences we may have in meditation: good and bad. Sometimes it is difficult to know which of the two is worse! We say this, facetiously of course, to highlight the fact that problems may arise from good meditation experiences as well as bad.

If at the start we have some dramatically good experiences, we may come to think of meditation as being *for* experiences. If these do not continue, we may begin to doubt our approach, ourselves or God. If we seem to have special success we may develop ego involvement in it. The good experience may precede our level of commitment by requiring more of us than we are ready to give, and we may become fearful of handling the power or the responsibility. Some "good" meditation periods may lure us astray short of the highest attunement of which we are capable even at the time. Although there are beautiful, reassuring and confirmatory experiences, these sometimes constitute special occasions to "test the spirits."

Beloved, believe not every spirit, but try the spirits whether they are of God.   I John 4:1

On the other hand, those experiences sometimes thought of as "bad" may be more instructive than they appear at first glance. Some, such as the feeling of an explosion in the head, may be part of the healing and attunement process. Many of the visions that John tells of in The Revelation which seem so catastrophic may be properly interpreted as part of the ongoing transformation process of his extensive healing experience. Other bad experiences may simply warn us of improper technique and thus be rather more instructive than destructive.

66

Some ask about the dangers of meditation. If meditation is understood to be practicing an awareness of His presence, it may be the safest and most saving activity in the world. Let us understand very clearly, then, that it is not meditation that is dangerous, but improper purpose and technique. Here, as much as in any phase of our lives, we must remember, "Make haste slowly, here a little, there a little, line upon line."

There is a tendency in man to perceive events that happen within as taking place outside himself. We can see this condition demonstrated in the frequency with which individuals have built altars or shrines at places where they have had transformative experiences. This is especially evident in stories of Old Testament characters. For example, we have seen how the tabernacle worship was an external projection of an internal process. The problem for man arises when he builds up rituals in the external world, expecting to re-create a particular experience. We need to realize that it is not the manipulation of elements of the exterior world that will bring an experience, but only becoming sincere in our search.

There is a tendency to translate inner events into outer ones. Warning one woman to be careful of this projective tendency, the readings instructed her to avoid seeing the goal of meditation as the achievement of an experience somewhere outside herself.

Q-4. Once when meditating on distant objects, I experienced the sensation of being unpleasantly suspended at a great height in the universe, with the result that for some time afterwards I feared the power of too effective a concentration of thought. Was there something wrong about the technique I used in trying to efface a sense of my physical ego?

A-4. Turn within, rather than holding to something above self. For know, the promise is that He shall meet thee within thine own temple. The technique, then, was in error. It is not above self, but within. For as ye raise the consciousness to that within self, He meeteth thee in thine own tabernacle, in the holy of holies; in the third eye—*not* above same!   1782-1

Many people have become frustrated with meditation because of their inability to have an experience of one kind or another. That which constitutes a good experience in meditation is difficult to judge. The only criterion that should be used to judge our own meditation is "the changed life." It is manifested in the fruits of the spirit: patience, kindness, faith, etc. The feeling of effective meditation is the feeling of love.

The following reading was given for a man who had limited himself by setting specific goals for himself based upon what he had heard others had experienced.

Q-6. [694]: Why don't I have more success with meditation?
A-6. Oft we find individual activity becomes so personal in even the meditations that there is sought that this or that, which may have been reported to have happened to another, *must* be the manner of happening to self. And in this manner there is cut away, there is built the barrier which prevents the real inner self from *experiencing.* Let self *loose,* as it were; for thy prayer ascends to the throne of grace, ever; only as self, though, metes out to thy fellow man. Do not *try,* or crave, or desire a sign; for *thou* art in *thyself* a sign of that thou dost worship within thine inner self!   705-2

A frequent question concerns out-of-body experiences. Certainly, such an experience may happen during meditation, and it is not something which should be feared. Nevertheless, if we understand the purpose for being in the earth, we can see that this is not something we should *try* to make happen. We meet God within—not out somewhere else.

> For this commandment which I command thee this day, it is not hidden from thee, neither is it far off. It is not in heaven, that thou shouldest say, Who shall go up for us to heaven, and bring it unto us, that we may hear it, and do it? Neither is it beyond the sea, that thou shouldest say, Who shall go over the sea for us, and bring it unto us, that we may hear it, and do it? But the word is very nigh unto thee, in thy mouth, and in thy heart, that thou mayest do it.   Deuteronomy 30:11-14

The Promises of Meditation

Although we have stressed the "hoping for nothing" (Luke 6:35) spirit of love as being basic to proper meditation, we are also given many promises which we are invited to claim.

> Prove me now herewith, saith the Lord of hosts, if I will not open you the windows of heaven, and pour you out a blessing, that there shall not be room enough to receive it.   Malachi 3:10

Specific promises of the beneficial effects of meditation are numerous in the Edgar Cayce readings. Summarized, they say that meditation properly practiced will make one stronger physically, mentally, emotionally, and spiritually, and consequently more able to be of help to others.

... seeing, feeling, experiencing of that image in the creative forces of love, enter into the Holy of Holies. As self feels or experiences the raising of this, see it disseminated through the inner eye (not the carnal eye) to that which will bring the greater understanding in meeting every condition in the experience of the body. Then listen to the music that is made as each center of thine own body responds to that new creative force that is being, and that is disseminated through its own channel: and we will find that little by little this entering in will enable self to renew all that is necessary—in Him . . .

. . . in meditation (when one has so purified self) that healing of every kind and nature may be disseminated on the wings of thought.   281-13

The magnitude of the potential effect of the regular practice of meditation cannot even be imagined. *The Secret of the Golden Flower* promises that meditation is so powerful a tool for spiritual growth that it can allow a man to move beyond the karmic patterns that would draw him back into the earth for a thousand incarnations.

If you only meditate for a quarter of an hour, by it you can do away with the ten thousand aeons and a thousand births. All methods end in quietness. This marvelous magic cannot be fathomed.   p. 33

Far and beyond these promises, however, the readings encourage us to read and claim as personally relevant all of the great promises of the Master. The Edgar Cayce information especially encourages us in the reading and personal acceptance of the assurances given in the 14th, 15th, 16th and 17th chapters of John. The A.R.E. book on this discourse given by Jesus, entitled *A Closer Walk,* should be the constant companion of every meditator practicing this approach. Here are some of the promises of the Master which should regularly inspire the meditator and of which we should constantly be assured.

. . . I am with you alway, even unto the end of the world.   Matthew 28:20

. . . Whosoever drinketh of the water that I shall give him shall never thirst; but the water that I shall give him shall be in him a well of water springing up into everlasting life.   John 4:14

This is the bread which cometh down from heaven, that a man may eat thereof, and not die.
I am the living bread which came down from heaven: if any man eat of this bread, he shall live for ever: and the bread that I will give is my flesh, which I will give for the life of the world.   John 6:50-51

Let not your heart be troubled: ye believe in God, believe also in me.

In my Father's house are many mansions: if it were not so, I would have told you. I go to prepare a place for you.

And if I go and prepare a place for you, I will come again, and receive you unto myself; that where I am, there ye may be also. John 14:1-3

I am the way, the truth, and the life: no man cometh unto the Father, but by me.

If ye had known me, ye should have known my Father also: and from henceforth ye know him, and have seen him. John 14:6-7

Verily, verily, I say unto you, He that believeth on me, the works that I do shall he do also; and greater works than these shall he do; because I go unto my Father.

And whatsoever ye shall ask in my name, that will I do, that the Father may be glorified in the Son.

If ye shall ask any thing in my name, I will do it.

If ye love me, keep my commandments.

And I will pray the Father, and he shall give you another Comforter, that he may abide with you forever;

Even the spirit of truth; whom the world cannot receive, because it seeth him not, neither knoweth him: but ye know him; for he dwelleth with you, and shall be in you.

I will not leave you comfortless: I will come to you. John 14:12-18

. . . when he, the Spirit of truth, is come, he will guide you into all truth: for he shall not speak of himself; but whatsoever he shall hear, that shall he speak: and he will shew you things to come. John 16:13

Behold, I stand at the door, and knock: if any man hear my voice, and open the door, I will come in to him, and will sup with him, and he with me.

To him that overcometh will I grant to sit with me in my throne, even as I also overcame, and am set down with my Father in his throne. Revelation 3:20-21

Chapter Five

THE PATTERN AND THE POWER

An implication of the concepts that we are children of God and made in His image is that we are miniature replicas of the universe. There is nothing in the universe that man can understand that doesn't have its representation within man himself. God made man as he is so that even in the limitations of three-dimensional consciousness man could come to an awareness of his oneness with Him. The realization of that awareness is dependent upon the choices that man makes in the utilization of the one creative energy, to which he has been given access. As man uses this energy, he imparts qualities of form to it. The formal or vibrational pattern that the energy takes on is determined by what is being held in the mind. Mind is the builder, and the thought patterns created by the mind can serve as a hindrance or as an aid to greater self-awareness, depending upon their nature. If they are in harmony with universal laws, they give life, love, and attunement.

At the fourth-dimensional level, man has access to every thought he has ever created (recall the relationship between the fourth dimension and an idea). His greatest responses of love and kindness have been recorded there, as well as the patterns of his greatest fears and resentments.

Jung's Concept of Archetypal Patterns

In addition to those patterns which have been personally created by an individual's mind throughout all of his experiences, each of us has access to patterns that are shared in common with all mankind. These impersonal or archetypal patterns are manifested in the dreams and the myths of all cultures. Many of the writings of Carl Jung refer to them. Differentiating between patterns based upon one's own unique experiences and those that are innate to all, Jung writes:

> A more or less superficial layer of the unconscious is undoubtedly personal. I call it the *personal unconscious*. But this personal unconscious rests upon

71

a deeper layer, which does not derive from personal experience and is not a personal acquisition but is inborn. This layer I call the *collective unconscious.* I have chosen the term "collective" because this part of the unconscious is not individual but universal; in contrast to the personal psyche, it has contents and modes of behavior that are more or less the same everywhere and in all individuals. It is, in other words, identical in all men and thus constitutes a common psychic substrate of a suprapersonal nature which is present in every one of us.

The contents of the collective unconscious are known as *archetypes.*

(*The Archetypes and the Collective Unconscious,* p. 3)

Jung's concept of the collective unconscious may not be directly correlated with the subconscious as Cayce described it; however, they are clearly similar. The readings indicate that all subconscious minds are in contact one with another. According to both concepts, the body provides the instrumentation, and the fourth-dimensional reality of the mind, as thoughts or ideas, provides the channel for the exchange of energy. The relationships may be diagramed as follows:

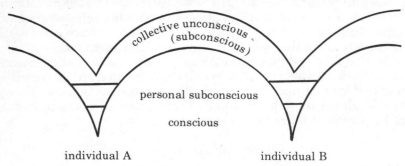

In his investigation of symbology, Lama Govinda comes to a conclusion similar to Jung's:

While mantric symbols have their origin within the cultural realm of a certain language or civilization, there are other symbols of figurative and conceptual nature, the origin of which cannot be traced to any particular place, tribe or race, and which are not bound to any particular period of human civilization or to any religion, but which are the common property of humanity. These symbols may disappear in one place— in fact they may be buried for centuries—only to reappear at another place, and to rise resurrected in a new and more brilliant garb. They may change their names and even their meaning, according to the emphasis laid upon the one or the other of their aspects, without losing their original direction: because it is in the nature of a symbol to be as manifold as the life from which it grew, and yet to retain its character, its organic unity within the diversity of its aspects.

(*Foundations of Tibetan Mysticism*, p. 51)

An example of an archetypal image is a dream, vision or symbolic representation of the lion or the great cat. In the Old Testament, Ezekiel had a vision in which he saw four beasts (or four cherubs, as he called them): a calf, a man, a lion and an eagle (Ezekiel 10:14). Similarly, in the New Testament, one of John's visions recounted in The Revelation includes the appearance of these same four beasts. Interpreting these visions, the Edgar Cayce readings indicate that they are specifically appropriate visual representations of structures and processes in the physical body. We may, for example, liken the visionary experience of the lion to the physiological activity of the adrenals. Seeing the image of a lion is likely to awaken in us a feeling of power and energy, which is related to the adrenal activities. Or, if there is particularly strong adrenal activity going on in the body, there may be an accompanying visualization, such as in a dream, of the lion or the great cat.

One man, in the midst of problems of resentment toward his wife, who had left him, dreamed that he was watching an activity on a stage while sitting in the front row of a theater. His feet extended forward so that they reached into a cage situated beneath the stage. He looked down and saw that within the cage there was a lion which was gnawing at his feet. This dream was an excellent portrayal of the pathological process that was taking place within him. The stage and its activity correspond to the conscious mind. Beneath this he became aware of the forces, symbolized by the lion, which were gnawing away within him. This dream is a precise description of the way in which continued resentment awakens within us a physiological and emotional process of the adrenals and of the way in which chronic stimulation of hormonal secretions sets up processes that gnaw away at the health of the body. In the dream, the disruptive situation was given visual representation in archetypal symbology related to the adrenal activity.

The archetype is related not only to the visual imagery, but also to the physical processes accompanying it. In other words, to appreciate fully a symbol we must realize that it can represent not only a pattern of energy in the subconscious mind, but also a condition, activity or response of the physical body. Commenting on the importance of understanding this dual nature of a symbol, Lama Govinda writes:

> A thing exists only insofar as it acts. Reality is actuality. An active symbol or image of spiritual vision is reality . . . A non-acting symbol or image is empty form, at the best a decorative construction or the remembrance of a concept, a thought, or an event, belonging to the past.
> (*Foundations of Tibetan Mysticism,* pp. 105-6)

Insofar as our culture places great value on or idolizes individual power, we worship it. Thus, in a symbolic sense, we can see the lion or the great cat as the totem or sacred animal of our times. We incorporate it into our lives because we want to possess its qualities. It is a matter of fact that if you put the likeness of a great cat on a product, it will sell. A tiger in the tank sells gasoline, Tony the tiger sells breakfast cereal, and a mountain lion on top of a sign sells automobiles. Advertising firms may not be interested in hearing about archetypal symbols, but they know that they work. Why do they work? The visual imagery triggers a specific and appropriate response system in the body. Almost universally, people agree that the great cats symbolize a kind of independent, controlled power, which is a greatly admired quality in our culture. Products bearing this image awaken within us an energy flow, associated with the solar plexus and the adrenal glands. We like the feeling of this flow; therefore, we want to possess such products, and we may come to worship them.

Another example of an archetypal image is the dream or vision of a bird. Often this takes the form of an eagle, as in the visions of Ezekiel and John. The Edgar Cayce readings interpret this symbol as being related to the activities of the heart center and the thymus gland. A clue to the psychological factor corresponding to this center is given in the description of the fourth Church in The Revelation, which the readings say is emblematic of the thymus center. The virtue of this Church is said to be charity or love, and the fault is fornication. If the activities of this center are out of balance, this quality can easily turn to concern, worry or jealousy. Often in language or symbolism we use the archetype of the bird when we wish to express this kind of attitude. For example, during the Vietnam war we applied the terms "hawks" and "doves" to two different types of concern. As another illustration, someone who is overly protective in a smotherly sort of way is often called a mother hen.

These examples point out that an archetype consists of both a visual experience and an accompanying physiological process related to the way in which we are made. We are all made in such a way that we are predisposed to having similar kinds of experiences. As miniature replicas of the universe, we have innumerable patterns within us which are found in other forms of life. We may think of a lion as biologically more capable of rage than a rabbit. When a response potential assumes a major role in the organizational hierarchy of our total functioning, its expression may be accompanied by recognizable archetypal symbols.

The Christ as an Archetype

One of the archetypal patterns in the unconscious of man is particularly consistent, in the qualities of its manifestations, with the original nature of the one creative energy. That nature is the life of good and of love; that pattern is the pattern of the Christ. The Christ pattern stands as an answer to the state of disunity with oneself, a condition that Jung refers to as "the hallmark of civilized man." We can think of neurosis as a state of divisiveness with the self in which different parts of a man are driving him towards contrary ends. A prevalent state of affairs for a man in our culture is to feel driven to do one thing by his analytical mind, to do another thing by his feelings or intuitions, and to do a third thing by the desires of his physical body. Illnesses of body and mind are the likely result of coping measures designed to deal symptomatically with this fragmentation.

In contrast to this we can identify a process within man that tends to draw together seemingly diverse elements of consciousness. The highest activity or function of man is to work towards a state of integration.

> Because intellect without feeling, knowledge without love, reason without compassion, leads to pure negation, to rigidity, to spiritual death, to mere vacuity—while feeling without reason, love without knowledge (blind love), compassion without understanding, lead to confusion and dissolution. But where both sides are united, where the great synthesis of heart and head, feeling and intellect, highest love and deepest knowledge have taken place, there completeness is re-established, perfect enlightenment is attained.   (*Foundations of Tibetan Mysticism,* p. 97)

On the one hand, this may be the integration of two conflicting drives or desires within a man, such as the hunger drive and the desire to have a slim, energetic physical body. An integrative pattern or archetype must function to bring together and not to exclude one factor in favor of another. A man functioning under such a pattern will find a diet that gives him sufficient amounts of food to satisfy his hunger and which is of a high enough nutritional quality to give him the energy he needs without gaining weight.

At a deeper level, this integrative process will be the union of the two seemingly contradictory polarities in the nature of man: the infinite and the finite. The work that God has for man to do in the earth is not a matter of choosing one nature to the exclusion of the other. Man is not to renounce his humanity to embrace an other-worldly concept of the Divine. In many ways such a choice would be the easy way out. The Christ pattern, the Christ archetype, is the process of integration which involves bringing the awareness of the infinite *into* the finite.

Then the purposes for which an entity enters material experience:
As indicated, the entity comes from without—or from an unknown quantity—into, first, that of desire, association, and conceptive activity with mental and physical growth, developing into a channel through which the spiritual import manifests.
Then its purpose is that such an entity, as this [1861], may make manifest the spiritual influence in a material world.
1861-4

This is simply living the law of love. This highest archetype within man can be described not only as a pattern, but as a law. It is within us not only in the sense that we can experience it visually, but in terms of a functioning of the entire body in a healing and integrating fashion. When we live by the law of love, which is giving, we initiate the activity of this archetype in every aspect of our lives. This pattern of functioning is available to all mankind. Jung argues that the rapid spread of Christianity is evidence to support his notion that the Christ is an element of the collective unconscious, and hence available to all.

Christ would never have made the impression He did on His followers if He had not expressed something that was alive and active in their unconscious. Christianity would never have spread through the pagan world with such astounding rapidity had its ideas not found an analogous psychic readiness to receive them. It is this

fact which also makes it possible to say that whoever
believes in Christ is not only contained in Him, but that
Christ then dwells in the believer as the perfect man
formed in the image of God . . .
(Jung, "Answer to Job," *Collected Works,*
Vol. 11, p. 441)

Finally, the Christ archetype is a pattern of healing. Man is
healed when all the aspects of himself are going in the same
direction. Of these aspects, there is one that has never lost
contact with the Godhead, and which is unchanging. In
contrast to this spiritual element of man, all other parts of
himself may be altered or may pass away. So if there is to be an
alignment, it will have to be in the direction towards which the
spiritual nature of man seeks to grow. Healing or integration
must be a step towards greater spiritual unfoldment. It is
towards this purpose that the Christ archetype works in the life
of man.

For as He has done ye may do, if ye live the life, if ye act in
that way as to bring that full awareness in all *phases* of the
urges within thy body, thy mind, thy soul being at one.
2608-1

In the Christ Consciousness, then, there is the oneness of
self, self's desires, self's abilities, made in at-onement with the
forces that may bring to pass that which is sought by an
individual entity or soul. 5749-4

Jesus Is the Pattern

For certain purposes, the Edgar Cayce readings make a
distinction between the Christ and Jesus. Although it has been
the tendency of many Christian theologians to use these names
synonymously, the readings suggest that we will form a better
understanding of ourselves by considering the difference
between these two words.

*Q-1. What is the meaning and significance of the words Jesus
and Christ . . . ?*
A-1. Just as indicated. Jesus is the man, the activity, the
mind, the relationships that He bore to others. Yea, He was
mindful of friends, He was sociable, He was loving, He was
kind, He was gentle, He grew faint, He grew weak—and yet
gained that strength that He has promised, in becoming the
Christ, by fulfilling and overcoming the world. You are made
strong, in body, in mind, in soul and purpose, by that power in
Christ. The *power,* then, is in the Christ. The *pattern* is in
Jesus. 2533-7

From the time of his creation there has existed within man the awareness of his own divine nature. Through the ages he has made choices that have built barriers between that universal state of consciousness and his own ego awareness. It was this process of self-imposed limitation that brought man to the point where he saw himself as primarily a physical body, with the mind little understood and the soul nearly forgotten. That pattern of love and integration which had always been a part of man's nature was contacted only by the few who had not totally encased their conscious awareness in thought patterns which were selfish and limiting. It was at this point in history that the Spirit of the Christ manifested in the world in the life of the man Jesus.

As man found himself out of touch with that complete consciousness of the oneness of God, it became necessary that the will of God, the Father, be made manifested, that a pattern be introduced into man's consciousness. Thus the son of man came into the earth, made in the form, the likeness of man; with body, mind, soul.   3357-2

The Wisdom then of the Lord thy God is shown thee, is exemplified to thee, is *patterned* for thee in the life of Jesus of Nazareth, Jesus the Christ!   262-104

The readings speak of Jesus as the *pattern* in two senses of the word. First, there is His relationship to that *state of consciousness* of the awareness of His oneness with the Godhead. This is the state of consciousness or the pattern that has always existed within man and which we can associate with the superconscious mind. Jesus lived in contact with this level of awareness and was one with the pattern in this sense. Equally important, He manifested His awareness in His relationship to the world around Him. By living out that high consciousness, He became the pattern in a second sense. The activities of His life and His approach to relationships of all kinds form a pattern that is the *key* to our individual attainment of the awareness of our true nature. In order to understand how it is the key, we need to recall the dual nature of any archetype. This consists of both a visual experience (related to the awareness or the consciousness) and an accompanying physical response (such as was exemplified in the activation of the adrenal glands).

Just as the experience of the symbol can result in the physiological response of the body, the presence of certain physical activities can lead to an experience of the symbol. As an example of the latter case, we have seen how prolonged periods of resentment and the accompanying adrenal activity can lead to the appearance of the image of the great cat in the dream life. In a similar fashion, if we will begin to act in selfless ways and thus put into action the physiological aspects of the Christ archetype, which would relate to the activities *and* the attitudes of the life of Jesus, the other aspect of the Christ pattern will begin to emerge: the conscious awareness of our oneness with God. It is important to remember that the active aspect of the archetype includes the attitude with which any action is carried out. Doing good deeds for outward show without having an attitude of love and genuine concern for others will not be enough to awaken higher consciousness.

The Nature of the Pattern

In the broadest sense, the nature of the Christ archetype is love. But in order to understand it more fully, it is helpful to look at some of the individual aspects or qualities of this pattern.
(1) It is relevant to human experience.
The first question that we must ask ourselves about the life of Jesus is, "Did He have to deal with the problems with which we have to deal now?" Some feel that we can dismiss the life and example of this man because He was evolved to such a point in His awareness that He was above the problems and concerns with which most of us have to work. In contrast to this, the Edgar Cayce readings suggest that Jesus did have to confront and make choices concerning every element of His own humanity. The pattern of His life answers every question about human experience.

In the urges, then, keep in that way ever of being a channel through which the greater amount of good may come to all, being—as the Master Himself—all things to all people; tempted in all points like each soul and yet without offense to any.
3395-2

Who *will* approach the Throne that ye may know that there is *none* that surpasses the Son of Man in His approach to *human* experience in the material world. 2897-4

(2) The pattern is established for all.
Just as with all archetypal patterns, the pattern of the life of Jesus exists at a level that is accessible to all mankind. This is not a matter of a man's beliefs; rather, it is related to certain laws about the nature of the mind. Just as we have access to the thought patterns of each other at the fourth-dimensional level

through the process called telepathy, so do we have access to that pattern built by the Master. We can think of this as a very real thing that exists in terms of energy and form. Like every other energy pattern created by the mind at the fourth-dimensional level, a man can choose to ignore it and deny its existence or to recognize it and allow it to manifest in his own life.

For the Master, Jesus, even the Christ, is the pattern for every man in the earth, whether he be Gentile or Jew, Parthenian or Greek. For all have the pattern, whether they call on that name or not ... 3528-1

(3) It manifests in the life of service.

The state of consciousness which we seek is the awareness of the unity of all being. An essential aspect of the nature of the Christ pattern is dealing with the world around us in such a way as to affirm the oneness that exists between ourselves and every other person and every element of nature. The life of service and the acceptance of responsibility in our relationships is such an affirmation. Being an aid to others in their growth is an integral part of our own growth.

And the entity will find more and more that, in that parlance—as may be said—that ye approach more and more to the very throne of grace, ye will find thyself leaning upon the arms of some to whom ye have shown those fruits of the spirit; to someone ye have comforted in trials, to someone you have fed—whether in the fruits of the spirit or in the needs of the body or the heart. These be those things that bring the consciousness of His abiding presence. 1493-1

The attainment of this state of salvation implies the overcoming of all narrow individual limitations and the recognition of super-individual realities within one's own mind. It is the most universal experience the human mind can attain, and from the very outset it demands a universal attitude; for he who strives for his own salvation, or merely with a view of getting rid of suffering in the shortest possible way, without regard for his fellow beings, has already deprived himself of the most essential means for the realization of his aim.
(*Foundations of Tibetan Mysticism,* p. 279)

(4) It sees God in every expression.

One of the fundamental premises of the Edgar Cayce readings is that there is only one energy or force in the universe.

This energy of the Godhead finds expression in many different forms, some of which have been created by man for selfish purposes. In essence, everything that we see is a manifestation of God. The pattern of Jesus is to see things at their deepest level and to relate to them in that way. To do otherwise is to separate life into those things which are of God and those which are of evil. It is sometimes difficult for a man to accept the principle that as he does unto the least of those around him, he is doing unto the whole, to God. This is the law and the nature of the pattern.

Hence there are laws immutable, unchanging. These are of spiritual import, yet are applicable in the experience of each entity in its dealings with its fellow man. That ye sow, that ye reap. As ye do unto thy fellow man, even the lowest in thine estimation, so ye do unto thy Maker. For the imprint, the soul, the spirit of each entity is a part of that great whole, that "I AM" by which the individual ego would seek to pattern itself...

The image of Him is within thine own self, if ye will but open thy heart, thy mind, thy conscience to the indwelling of that force, of that promise which is thine own—if ye will but embrace same.   1796-1

Which is more real, the love manifested in the Son, the Savior, for His brethren, or the essence of love that may be seen even in the vilest of passion? They are one.   254-68

Similarly, Lama Govinda, writing of the qualities of the consciousness of enlightenment, states that one of the principles which we must understand is the oneness that lies behind seeming dualities.

> ... the highest qualities are potentially contained in the lower ones (like the blossom in the seed). Thus, good and bad, the sacred and the profane, the sensual and the spiritual, the worldly and the transcendental, ignorance and enlightenment, samsara and nirvana, etc., are not absolute opposites, or concepts of entirely different categories, but two sides of the same reality.
> (*Foundations of Tibetan Mysticism,* pp. 107-8)

The great Greek novelist Nikos Kazantzakis illustrates this same aspect of the Christ pattern in a story about St. Francis of Assisi. For years St. Francis had become afraid at the sight of a leper, but he came to the realization that he had to accept this challenge that God had placed before him and love and embrace even such an ugly person. While he was walking to the

81

city, a leper appeared along the road, and St. Francis was finally able to see the inner essence of such a diseased body.

Half of his putrescent nose had fallen away; his hands were without fingers—just stumps; and his lips were an oozing wound.
Throwing himself upon the leper, Francis embraced him, then lowered his head and kissed him upon the lips.

St. Francis then covered him with his robe and they began to walk together towards the city. They walked for several hours, until they were nearly to its gates.

Suddenly I saw Francis stop abruptly. He bent down and drew aside the robe in order to uncover the leper. But all at once he uttered a loud cry: the robe was empty!
The tears flowing from his eyes, he fell prostrate on the ground and began to kiss the soil. I remained standing above him, trembling. It wasn't a leper, it was Christ Himself who had come down to earth in the form of a leper in order to test Francis.

(*St. Francis*, pp. 94-5)

The same principle pertains to the way in which we relate to the various parts of ourselves. Since the Christ pattern involves a process of integration, we must be willing to accept even the most unwanted parts of ourselves. To see the good in that which we would prefer to hide from ourselves and others is a difficult task. Carl Jung writes that such a capacity to see the Christ in even the least commendable parts of ourselves is necessary to mental health.

In actual life it requires the greatest art to be simple, and so acceptance of oneself is the essence of the moral problem and the acid test of one's whole outlook on life. That I feed the beggar, that I forgive an insult, that I love my enemy in the name of the Christ—all these are undoubtedly great virtues. But what I do unto the least of my brethren, that I do unto Christ. But what if I should discover that the least amongst them all, the poorest of all beggars, the most impudent of all offenders, yea the very fiend himself—that these are within me, that I myself stand in need of the alms of my own kindness, that I myself am the enemy that must be loved, what then?

(*Modern Man in Search of a Soul*, p. 235)

Jesus said, "It is I; be not afraid." (John 6:20) We must grow to the awareness of seeing Him in everything and everyone. Thus we turn stumbling blocks into stepping-stones.

(5) It is obedient to higher law.

In a culture where we prefer to talk of personal freedom and "doing your own thing," the concept of obedience is quickly tossed aside. Yet, how can we become one with ourselves if we are unwilling to do what we know we ought to do? Too easily we fall into the notion that we are not enlightened because we are trapped by exterior laws or rules of behavior. While it may be true that man can limit himself by constrictive rules or morals, diet and other forms of human behavior, the fact remains that the universe is governed by certain immutable laws. One aspect of the nature of the Christ pattern is related to the way in which Jesus responded to His knowledge of these universal laws. Man becomes one with the law only as he is joyfully obedient to it.

Hence we find, as the Son represents the mind of self, it is then necessary that each soul choose the being of one mind with Him—who thought it not robbery to make Himself equal with God, and who hath called to *every* one, "Be ye perfect, even as my Father in heaven is perfect."

What (ye ask) has this to do with the trials, the temptations, the disappointments that have come into the experience of every individual at one period or another?

Learn, even as it was said of Him; that though He were the Son, even *He* learned obedience through the things which *He* suffered. 2427-1

One of the fundamental laws to which man must be obedient is his own nature as a spiritual being. We must be obedient to the fact that we are divine, and our refusal to accept the validity of this idea often causes us to suffer. Such suffering can be used as a learning mechanism. Often, in such a state, man is forced to reach deeply within himself to find new strengths in order to get through these periods. Capacities and levels of awareness that otherwise might remain unknown break forth into consciousness because of the great need. In this way, suffering can become a stepping-stone to greater self-awareness.

Remember rather the pattern as was manifested for thee in the Son; how that though He were the Son, yet learned He obedience through the things which He suffered.

He used, then, that which was necessary in the experience in the earth as periods of suffering, as periods of rejection, even by His own that He had called, that were His friends; not as stumbling stones but as stepping-stones to make for thee, for the world, that access for each soul, for the closer relationship of the Father, through the Son, to the children of men. 2600-2

(6) It is joyous.

The readings stress that Jesus was not a solemn or joyless person. An important aspect of His pattern is the capacity to laugh with life and with oneself, even in times of trouble.

Cultivate the ability to see the ridiculous, and to retain the ability to laugh. For, know—only in those that God hath favored is there the ability to laugh, even when clouds of doubt arise, or when every form of disturbance arises. For, remember, the Master smiled—and laughed, oft—even on the way to Gethsemane.   2984-1

(7) It is compassionate.

One of the most common complaints in our times is "No one understands me." Such feelings of alienation and separateness are the result of being out of contact with the level of one's being where the fundamental oneness is perceived. It is the nature of the Christ pattern to accept responsibility for helping one's neighbor when he is in such a state, and one way to do this is with sympathy. Sympathy, meaning "to feel with another," involves not only an acceptance of where another person is in consciousness, but a willingness to move in one's own awareness in order to experience that feeling with him.

For He wept with those who wept, and rejoiced with those who rejoiced.   2995-1

Accepting such a concept may be difficult for some who prefer to think that the spiritually enlightened person is able to remain strong and detached from the display of feelings of those around him. Much has been made of the relative desirability of empathy as opposed to sympathy, because the former involves an attempt to understand the internal state of another without experiencing his feelings or emotions with him. Certainly it is true that it would be very difficult to maintain a state of mental balance if one were constantly trying to experience the emotions of others. In the Christ pattern there is a sensitivity and a knowing as to when such a sympathetic response is necessary as an aid to the spiritual growth of another. With the desire to be of service to others there will come a psychic sensitivity which will often meet the need that may arise to understand the emotional and mental workings of another. Sympathy is a part of the Christ pattern as it is used for others and not for emotional self-indulgence. Often it takes the wisdom of the Christ for us to know for which purpose we are using it.

There are instances where we express love by moving in

awareness to where another who is in need finds himself. This principle is illustrated in a story related by Rosalind Heywood, who has been called "the mother of parapsychology." In her book, *ESP: A Personal Memoir,* she describes an experience that came to her while she was in a heightened, altered state of consciousness. While in this state she was shown what it was like for those individuals who were schizophrenic.

> And terrible it was. At its furthest point I came on a cold, grey, stony, El Greco-like desert, its monotony broken only by jagged rocks. There was not a leaf to be seen anywhere, not a blade of grass. Huddled far apart among the rocks were grey veiled figures, motionless, unable to communicate, "at the bottom," beyond despair. They were, I knew, the Lost. I have never before or since felt the total compassion I felt then. I remember pausing by one of them and thinking desperately, "Is there nothing I can do to rouse and comfort him?"
>
> And the answer was—nothing. I could make no contact. I was not good enough. None less, it appeared, that the perfectly Good could help the Lost, and to do so they had to sink in sacrifice, even below them, to become the objects of their pity and compassion. It was only by giving those at the bottom a chance to help others who needed it that they could be saved. And by some strange paradox only the perfectly Good could get below them to need their love.
>
> (*ESP: A Personal Memoir,* pp. 209-10)

(8) It lives in the present.

There is that within man which says, "I am." It is always here and is always in the now. It is difficult for man in a three-dimensional consciousness that divides time into past, present, and future to understand that his consciousness is in the eternal now. To His contemporaries who awaited the establishment of a divine order in the earth at some unspecified point in the future, Jesus' message was that at that very moment the kingdom of God (as a consciousness) was available to everyone who would but choose it.

> In the material associations, in the material connections, then, do with thy might what thy hand finds to do *today.* For sufficient unto the day is the good as well as the evil thereof. For as He hath given in thee that thou may be a channel, the representative, the agent—yea, the very representative in flesh of Him, then act in thine inner self, act in thine outward expression, as though thou wert (for thou art!) His child, and

are heir to all the glories *here, now,* of His kingdom. *Not* in the future, not in the past! For in the eternal *now* is He *active* in thee.   683-2

(9) It is forgiving.

In the Biblical account of Jesus' giving the Lord's Prayer to His disciples, He comments afterwards on only one section of the prayer:

> For if ye forgive men their trespasses, your heavenly Father will also forgive you; but if ye forgive not men their trespasses, neither will your Father forgive you your trespasses.   Matthew 6:14-15

We may assume that the Master felt that this aspect of the pattern deserved special attention or consideration. Perhaps this is because historically man's attempts to reach God had been so closely tied to sacrifice and not to mercy. It has been suggested that sacrifice was once used to free souls that had projected into matter in animal form and had become trapped; the practice carried on even after such projections had ceased.

The practice of sacrifice is only a misunderstanding of how to deal with the realization that purification is necessary. It is true that we need to stop feeding thought patterns which are of a limiting nature and, in that sense, to sacrifice our involvement with them. The problem arises when man projects what is an inner process onto the outer world. For example, we realize that a tendency to be rude cuts us off from the consciousness of love, and so we attempt to reject rudeness in our expression. But the rejection or the sacrifice is all too often attempted through a critical or unforgiving attitude towards another person in whom we see this characteristic. Jesus teaches that what God asks from man is mercy, not sacrifice. The Christ pattern is integrative in nature. It tends to bring all the aspects of oneself together, so that the confused or inharmonious ones may be lifted up and healed. This is exactly what we do when we choose to forgive ourselves and others. Forgiveness is an affirmation that purification can be achieved more effectively by accepting shortcomings and trusting that they can be healed in this spirit of love.

For as each individual realizes, as these tenets may be analyzed, if God had condemned—what opportunity would there be for man to find his way back to God? Thus each individual must do unto others as he would have his Brother, the Christ, his God, the Father, do unto him; and indeed, then, apply first, last and always His "Forgive, O God, as I forgive others. Find fault in me, O God, as I find fault in my brother."

5758-1

For, "As ye would that men should do to you, do ye even so to them" is the law; not merely of sacrifice, not merely of recompense but of grace and mercy—which are so sought for by the entity in the assurances of that "As ye would be forgiven, so must ye forgive"; for "As ye do it unto the least of thy brethren, ye do it unto thy Maker" is the spiritual law.

1492-1

(10) It is patient.

Recall that as one of the three dimensions in man's experience, patience is the measure of one's understanding of the *purpose* of manifested ideas. That purpose is that man would show forth in his daily life the pattern that is shown in Jesus, that he might become aware of the reality of his being.

Yet, as was given in those admonitions by Him—who in the flesh was a manifestation, or became the manifestation of the God-consciousness in the material world—"In patience ye may become aware of, or awaken to, thy soul. In patience, and living in that consciousness, I may bring to your remembrance all things from the foundations of the world."

2246-1

(11) It stresses the spirit in which we act.

It has long been recognized that there is a relationship between the actions of a man and his inner state of awareness. Spiritual teachers for ages have tried to make use of this correspondence in order to help others reach particular levels of consciousness. There is a third factor that is an integral part of this process, and it has often been misunderstood or ignored; it is the importance of the attitude or the spirit in which the action is conducted.

There are many popular consciousness-altering movements in our culture today. Many individuals may have experienced heightened states of awareness by practicing specific techniques and rules taught in such courses. Some of these procedures, or analogous ones related to various activities of the mind and body, have been practiced for thousands of years.

Throughout the experience of man in the material world, at various seasons and periods, teachers or "would-be" teachers have come; setting up certain forms or certain theories as to manners in which an individual shall control the appetites of the body or of the mind, so as to attain to some particular phase of development.

357-13

In contrast to this we have the pattern of Jesus, which is not concerned with rules or techniques, but emphasizes instead the spirit in which one lives. When our actions are motivated by the spirit of love, we can trust that they will be of such a nature as to awaken higher levels of consciousness. Carrying out rules or disciplines that are likely to alter one's consciousness does not guarantee that one will be able to operate with greater love and sensitivity at that new level of consciousness. It is a matter of what we put first in our lives—the affirmation that we are spiritual beings (hence, concern for purposes) or the belief that we are physical beings (hence, preoccupation with techniques and rules of conduct).

The reading continues:

There has also come a teacher who was bold enough to declare himself as the son of the living God. He set no rules of appetite. He set no rules of ethics, other than, "As ye would that men should do to you, do ye even so to them," and to know "Inasmuch as ye do it unto the least of these, thy brethren, ye do it unto thy Maker." He declared that the kingdom of heaven is within each individual entity's consciousness, to be attained, to be aware of—through meditating upon the fact that God is the Father of every soul. 357-13

(12) It is humble.

The nature of the Christ pattern is the union of the infinite and the finite. But that integration within man can be achieved only as the finite, physical consciousness becomes aware of its limitations and surrenders itself to the purposes and will of the infinite spirit within. It is not that the finite man would seek to grasp at the infinite and pull himself into it; instead, it is that he would humble himself and allow the infinite to interpenetrate his finitude. In this way is the spirit brought *into* the earth.

We must claim that consciousness that God is our Father, that we were made in His image to be companions and co-creators with Him; however, in so doing we must also assume the attitude of Jesus, who humbled Himself and became obedient unto death. That attitude realizes that only God is Good; that we are merely channels through which the Spirit may flow; that it is not we who do good works, but only the Father in us; that we, of ourselves, can do nothing; and that he who would be greatest must be the servant of all.

Humility is understanding the relationship between one's conscious physical self in the material world and the invisible forces of the soul. The opposite of humility is self-aggrandizement, in which there is a twisting of the truth that man has a divine nature; the result is an attitude that seeks to grasp at the infinite, instead of being grasped and transformed by it.

88

Humility should not be conceived of as self-degradation, but instead as an attitude of self-understanding and self-acceptance which permits man to fulfill his purpose for being in the finite, material world.

Then in thine own self there are the needs to humble thyself before thy fellow man; not as one ashamed. Because the Master was humble before the throng, the mockery, the rulers, the riffraff, and wore the purple robe and the crown of thorns, was He ashamed of His position?

Then humbleness is not being ashamed but rather as He, *knowing* in self that it is that necessary for God's will to be the better, the more perfectly, the more truly manifested in thine own experience!   1440-2

He Is Thy Karma

In a sense, we can think of karma as the energizing of patterns which have been built by the mind at the fourth-dimensional level. As an example, for a better understanding of how karma works, consider a device that we might construct to illustrate the way in which these patterns can affect life in the material world. Let this device be basically a cassette tape player, but built in such a way that many individual cassette tapes may be loaded into it at once, similar to the way in which records are placed in a juke box. We shall construct this tape player so that the cassette tapes are stacked one on top of another. When a starter button is pushed, one of the tape cartridges is automatically inserted into the playing mechanism and whatever is on the tape is heard. This device is built so that the nearer a tape is to the top of the stack, the more likely it is that it will be selected by the machine for playing. Selections may be made automatically, by buttons pushed by other people, or by choices made by ourselves, overriding the other selection devices.

Now let us recall an instance from our experiences in which someone did something to us and we responded immediately without thinking. Many of us have experienced being shoved, and the immediate response is often to push back or to strike the person responsible. In the analogy, someone has pushed our starter button and whatever response pattern or cassette tape is nearest the top of the stack is the one most likely to be selected and played—that is, manifested as our physical and emotional response. Often there is a stimulus from the outside world to which we react automatically. Later we say, "I don't know what came over me; I didn't mean to do that." The alternative to automatic reactive behavior is to begin to work with rearranging the hierarchy or the order in which these cassette tapes are stacked within us—to place those patterns associated with loving and creative expression at the top. We do this by the way that we focus our attention (remember, mind is the builder), because when the attention is placed upon any pattern two things happen. First, we energize that fourth-dimensional pattern (or cassette tape) and invite it to project or express itself in the three-dimensional reality of our material lives. Second, we change its position within the mind, putting it into a place that makes it more likely to manifest in the future, even when an immediate, reactive response is demanded.

The analogy of a tape recording is a particularly instructive one for understanding the nature of karma. Karmic patterns are memories in much the same way that sounds recorded magnetically on tape are memories. Just as playing a tape recording does not erase it, living through a karmic experience does not necessarily rid us of our involvement with that pattern which brought on the experience. Karma is commonly referred to in terms of a debt. But there is a way in which this is easily misunderstood and the very nature of the growth process for man is ignored. Man grows in awareness only as he accepts responsibility for his own status as a co-creator with God. A karmic experience is a challenge to a man to consider a choice that he has once made or an attitude that he has once held, and to see that it was founded upon a misunderstanding of the laws of the universe. Until it is seen in this light and a way more in accord with the law of love is chosen, that pattern previously built remains as a hindrance to growth. Meeting karma is not just letting the tape play, but working with new insights, constructive attitudes and helpful purposes, and with a sense of personal responsibility as a difficult situation unfolds in our lives.

We are not dealing with a God who is vengeful and who demands punishment for each transgression. In a sense, to believe such a thing is to look for an easy way out. Our situation is like that of a child who breaks a rule by sneaking cookies from the cookie jar between meals; we are not just to learn to put up with the resulting spanking that we receive (i.e., the payment of a debt), but instead we must come to understand why the rule exists and learn to live obediently within it. It is often far more difficult for a man to accept responsibility for his past, to see beyond his limited perspectives, and to change his behavior than it is to take a punishment that supposedly evens things out.

For example, a man who in one lifetime chooses to mutilate a physical body (his own or another's) may require of himself more than just one subsequent life in which he is physically impaired (i.e., to pay back the debt). Instead, it may take several lifetimes in such a state for him to come to the realization that the body is the temple and should be treated with love and respect. The important thing is not that the punishment be taken, but that there be a change in consciousness. We move out of our involvement with these limiting patterns that we have created only as we choose to place a pattern of greater love in a position of higher priority in our lives.

Such a pattern is the one we have in Jesus. Although this pattern of love has always existed within us, through the life of Jesus we were given greater access to it. In this sense, His work was at the fourth-dimensional level. In the model of the mind of man that we have, the life of Jesus is depicted as a movement of the pattern of love from the superconscious into the subconscious.

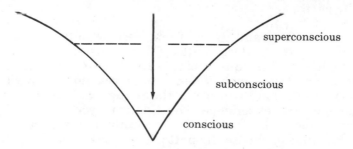

In the Biblical account, this is symbolized by the rending of the veil of the temple at His death. This veil was located between the inner court, corresponding to the subconscious, and the holy of holies, corresponding to the superconscious.

> The entity finds self a body, a mind, a soul... These are as the shadows which were indicated in the mount by the outer court (the body), the inner court (the mind), and the still more holy of holies (the soul). These are but shadows, and yet indicate the trend of the development...
>
> 2067-1

Until the time of Jesus, the subconscious memory patterns of man proved a formidable barrier to any attempt by man's physical conscious mind to contact the superconscious level. In order to build the pattern at a level closer to man in his physical consciousness, Jesus had to contend with all the thought forms that mankind had collected at the fourth-dimensional level. To establish the pattern in a place so accessible to man, Jesus had to deal with all the other patterns that were already there. Because this work was being done for mankind collectively, He had to deal with not just His own fourth-dimensional thought patterns, but those of everyone. In this way, we can say that Jesus took on the sins (the karmic memories) of the world. We have all experienced the principle that lies behind the necessity of His taking on these patterns. When you put something in a new place, you must deal with what is already there. If you move into a new home, you can expect to have to deal with your new neighbors—to become involved in the interplay of the community. It was only by facing every temptation offered by the various thought patterns created by mankind that Jesus could make the manifestable pattern more accessible to man.

Though man be far afield, then, though he may have erred, there is established that which makes for a closer, closer walk with Him, through that One who experienced all those turmoils, strifes, desires, urges that may be the lot of man in the earth.   5749-6

Attunement and grace, then, become only a matter of our *choosing* the pattern built by Jesus, instead of the others to which we have equal access. In a sense, they are all there together at the fourth-dimensional level, but it is only by an act of will that man can bring the pattern of love into his three-dimensional experience. The Edgar Cayce readings are very clear about the fact that we cannot make excuses for our reluctance to choose the pattern of Jesus either by pointing to hindrances created by the world around us or by blaming our parents for the genetic influences they have given us.

Q-15. Are heredity, environment and will equal factors in aiding or retarding the entity's development?
A-15. Will is the greater factor, for it may overcome any or all of the others; provided that will is made one with the pattern, see? For, no influence of heredity, environment or whatnot, surpasses the will; else why would there have been that pattern shown in which the individual soul, no matter how far astray it may have gone, may enter with Him into the holy of holies?   5749-14

It is by using this will that we awaken from within the Christ Consciousness.

Q-18. Should the Christ Consciousness be described as the awareness within the soul, imprinted in pattern on the mind and waiting to be awakened by the will, of the soul's oneness with God?
A-18. Correct. That's the idea exactly!   5749-14

92

The Christ Consciousness is an *awareness* of our oneness with God that comes from within. It exists in the form of a pattern in the mind (i.e., at the fourth-dimensional level). It is brought to the conscious awareness of man only as he uses his will and chooses that pattern as the ideal. Then the mind, beginning in meditation, uses that spiritual ideal to build upon until we move from awareness in the Christ Consciousness to fulfillment in the Christ Spirit.

This is what is involved if we would contact the consciousness of the Master. It is not a matter of having a spirit guide or knowing a particularly attuning chant or participating in rigorous disciplines of body and mind. It is a matter of choosing, awakening, building, living and becoming the life of balance and of love as exemplified in Jesus.

Q-8. [379]: How may I raise my vibrations so as to contact the Christ?
A-8. Making the will, the desire of the heart one with His ...
5749-4

Q-4. Is Jesus the Christ on any particular sphere or is He manifesting on the earth plane in another body?
A-4. ... not in a body in the earth, but may come at will to him who *wills* to be one with, and acts in love to make same possible.
5749-4

If we think of karma as the energizing of patterns that the mind has built at the fourth-dimensional level, we can understand one of the most remarkable statements from the Edgar Cayce readings.

What *is* karma? and what *is* the pattern?
He alone is each soul pattern. He *alone* is each soul pattern! *He* is thy *karma,* if ye put thy trust *wholly* in Him!   2067-2

... *know* that thy body is the temple of the *living* God; *there* ye may seek communion! There ye may seek counsel as to the choices to be made, the directions to be taken!
Thus does He—as in His promise, "Lo, I am with thee always, unto the end"—*become* thy way, and become that termed by some thy karma.
622-6

If we will choose to make it so, our experience in the material world will be a product of our involvement with the pattern of Jesus and not with the patterns of selfishness and limitation that are so often chosen.

For if you will read the Book of Revelation with the idea of the body as the interpretation, you will understand yourself and learn to really analyze, psychoanalyze, mentally analyze others. But you will have to learn to apply it in self first. For the motivating force in each one of those patterns represented, is that which the individual entity entertains as the ideal. This is the motivating spirit, the motivating purpose. When it is out of attune, or not coordinating with the First Cause, there may not be the greater unfoldment. For it is in self that it becomes out of attune. It loses its power or ability. It loses creative energy or its hold upon the First Cause that is the Creator or God.

Through what channels do these approach the activity? Through mind! Mind as a stream, not mind as purely physical or as wholly spiritual, but it is that which shapes, which forms, which controls, which directs, which builds, which acts upon.

4083-1

Each one of us is challenged personally to decide what we will do with the opportunity that is given to choose the life of love and of self-understanding.

What, then, will you do with Jesus?
For He is the Way, He is the Light, He is the Hope, He *is* ready. Will you let Him into thy heart? or will you keep Him afar or apart? Will ye not eat of His body, of the bread of life? Drink from that fountain that He builds in the minds, the hearts, the souls of those that seek to know Him and His purposes with men, with the world!

For having overcome the world, He *indeed* has it—as it were—in the palm of His hand; and has entrusted to you this world, because of His faith, His love for you.

What will you do about Jesus and His trust *in you?* 254-95

Chapter Six

IDEALS

If we have set our will and mind upon spiritual growth, the first step is the setting of the spiritual ideal. In making such a conscious choice of a standard and a direction for our lives, we are providing for ourselves that which for a house is the foundation, for a ship is the rudder, for a navigator is the North Star and for the mason is the plumb line. The ideal gives us a sense of stability, guidance and orientation, as well as a criterion for judgments. Without these the work of self-exploration and integration can quickly become overwhelming. For this reason the Edgar Cayce readings stress the paramount importance of setting a spiritual ideal.

Then, the more important, the most important experience of this or any entity is to first know what *is* the ideal—spiritually.
357-13

Similarly, Lama Govinda points out that we can never really become aware of the totality of our inner capabilities unless we are willing constantly to set our sights upon the highest understanding that we have in the present. The man that sets his mind on the greatest truth that he has experienced and goes about trying to become one with that truth is the one who will experience a spiritual awakening, enabling him to grow beyond his present limitation.

Just as an artist will hold before himself the greatest masters as worthy examples, irrespective of whether he will be able to reach their perfection or not, thus, whosoever wants to progress spiritually, must turn towards the highest ideal within the range of our understanding. This will urge him to ever higher achievements. For nobody can say from the beginning, where the limits of one's capacities are—in fact, it is more probable that it is the intensity of our striving that determines these limits. He who strives for the highest, will partake of the highest forces, and thereby he himself will move his limits into the infinite: he will realize the infinite in the finite, making the finite the vessel of infinity, the temporal the vehicle of the timeless.

(*Foundations of Tibetan Mysticism,* pp. 45-46)

If we are not concerned with the motivational basis from which we are operating, then it is useless to consider what we might set for ourselves as an ideal. A sense of direction is important only to the one who seeks a particular destination. Otherwise, there is little reason to do more than just accept those experiences that come to us and make do with the consciousness that arises from them. If we have set our sights upon experiencing the awareness of our oneness with God, then we have reason to look for an orientation that will be likely to lead to that. The first step that the Edgar Cayce readings recommend is to decide exactly what (or, rather, in Whom) it is that one believes.

Shall we be like Alice:

Alice: Chesire Puss, would you tell me which way I ought to go from here?
Puss: That depends a good deal on where you want to get to.
Alice: I don't much care where . . .
Puss: Then it doesn't matter which way you go.

(*Alice in Wonderland*)

Or shall we follow the advice given in this passage:

Know who is the author of thy beliefs, as well as of what ye believe. And unless these be founded upon Creative Forces that take hold upon God Himself, is it worthy of thought, meditation? 1765-2

The inner transformation can occur only through that which Lama Govinda calls "turning about in the deepest seat of consciousness." This is achieved by focusing the attention upon the inner spiritual reality, as opposed to the demands of the outer, material world. In the Bible it is more than John the Baptist saying, "Repent"; it is the prodigal son saying, "I will arise and go to my father." In the language of the readings, this is the setting of a spiritual ideal. The first step towards spiritual awakening is not contained in an obscure or esoteric teaching. It is simply a matter of choosing a foundation and direction, a quality of motivation, from which all growth can come.

It is the re-orientation, the new attitude, the turning away from the outside world of objects to the inner world of oneness, of completeness—the all-embracing universality of the mind. It is a new vista, "a direction of the heart" (as Rilke calls it), an entering into the stream of liberation. It is the only miracle which the Buddha recognized as such and beside which all other *siddhis* are mere playthings.

(*Foundations of Tibetan Mysticism,* p. 75)

Q-7. What ideal is meant in the statement, "by keeping an ideal, *not an idea, an ideal, before self"?*
A-7. An ideal means that to which the entity may, itself, ever look up, knowing itself to be gradually becoming a portion, but *never* **may it be the whole. Something to look up to, or to attempt to** *attain* **to; not an idea, that I may do this or I may do that, that I may accomplish such and such through such modes of operation! for then one reaches the goal! An ideal is that as is sought by, and developed to be, at an at-onement with same, a portion of same, but never the whole.** 256-2

When we say the word *ideal,* many may think of the word *goal.* American society, which has grown out of philosophic pragmatism, scientific materialism, and industrial productivity, is particularly goal-oriented. When we concern ourselves with the outcome of some course of action, we miss the whole point of the spiritual life. An ideal does not mean a goal. Rather, it is concerned with the motive, purpose, intention—in sum, the spirit in which we do whatever we have to do. Clearly, two men can do the same work; yet, one can have a loving, constructive, appreciative attitude, and the other a selfish, ego-oriented outlook. Although the finished products may look the same, that which has happened inside these two individuals is entirely different. The Way lies in doing whatever our hands find to do in His spirit of love.

Choosing to work with an ideal is being willing to be primarily concerned with the purpose behind an activity. Action is to be carried out in such a way that our attitude while we work will be in accord with our ideal. Our first concern is not so much for the "what" of our activities (e.g., what will the boat that I'm going to build look like?); instead, we concern ourselves with the "why" and the "how" (e.g., I'm going to build that boat in order that others will have a means of transportation; and I'm going to do the work with an attitude of love and service). Clearly this order of thinking will lead to a more satisfactory outcome, even at the goal level.

Ours is the opportunity to choose the standard and direction by which we as individuals want to guide our lives. Growth in meditation is tied directly to the way in which we make effective use of our will to turn our awareness towards the motivational realities of the inner life.

> To be born as a human being is a privilege, according to Buddha's teaching, because it offers the rare opportunity of liberation through one's own decisive effort, through a "turning about in the deepest seat of consciousness."
>
> *(Foundations of Tibetan Mysticism,* p. 124)

Writing Down Ideals

The Edgar Cayce readings recommend very strongly that each of us write our ideals down. By rising to this simple task we meet one of the great spiritual challenges of earthly experience. Every reason that arises in our mind for not taking this manifest step may be scrutinized closely and found to be a rationalized resistance to being specific and decisive about our "turning about."

A written analysis has a quality of stability which a vague mental notion does not provide. When the time for decision arrives, the carefully written criterion becomes a genuine help in keeping ourselves oriented toward our chosen direction of growth. Equally important is the confirming record of that growth over time as we come to rethink and rewrite those ideals into even higher expressions.

The Spiritual Ideal

Archimedes, the Greek mathematician of the third century B.C., is purported to have said, "Give me a lever long enough and I can move the world." This is theoretically possible, if one can find a stable fulcrum or pivot point on which the rigid bar can rest.

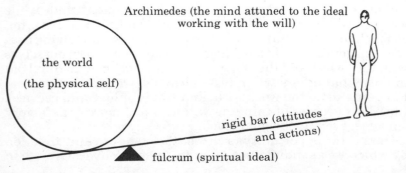

Archimedes (the mind attuned to the ideal working with the will)

the world

(the physical self)

rigid bar (attitudes and actions)

fulcrum (spiritual ideal)

We need a place to stand, a place to which to return, a sense of stability, a way of getting *centered*. As we set that for ourselves, we can say, "Here is something in which I have confidence and faith." Having set such a center, we have a point of reference to which we can return when we are assailed by doubts, confusion, discouragement or temptation. Spiritual stability comes into our lives as we become willing to invest in it. We need not wait until some revelation suddenly descends upon us or some great religious experience comes along. We can start where we are and establish our center for ourselves. From that point we can then begin to grow.

The readings suggest that we choose the one word that for us represents such a stable place to stand—a motivational quality by which we are willing to measure our lives. This is not a word that someone else would require of us; it is not something that we have read about in a book or have heard about in church; it is, instead, a word that for us would constitute a spiritual ideal.

. . .thy spiritual concept of the ideal, whether it be Jesus, Buddha, mind, material, God or whatever is the word which indicates to self the ideals spiritual.   5091-3

The most important thing we can do—in whatever situation we find ourselves—is to choose the word that awakens in us the spirit of the highest that we know. What is the one word that calls forth from us the spirit in which we want to live our lives, the spirit that we would like to have motivating us?

One reason that setting the spiritual ideal is so vitally important is that everything we perceive in the material world has as its basis some spiritual ideal. All physical manifestations have their origins in mental patterning, and those mental patterns are founded upon the impulse of a spiritual ideal.

First, know thy ideals, physical, mental, and spiritual. And know the physical result is first conceived in spirit, acted upon by mind, and then manifested in the material—with what spirit ye entertain.   2813-1

Mental Ideals

Once we have specified the spiritual ideal, the next step is to decide upon the relationships in our lives which we want to work on to improve, such as those with our family, job, friends, church, etc. The mental aspect of the ideal consists of the attitudes that we hold toward these relationships. With each relationship we are to ask the question, "What attitude is awakened in my mind in regard to this area of my life when I say the one word that I have chosen as my spiritual ideal?" The answer may be more than one particular attitude, and some attitudes may be applicable to several different aspects of our lives.

. . .write the ideal *mental* attitude, as may arise from the concepts of the spiritual, [in the] relationship to self, to home, to friends, to neighbors, to thy enemies, to things, to conditions.   5091-3

It is clear that the mental ideal rests upon the spiritual ideal. The mental ideal and the physical ideal are derived from the spiritual. More accurately, they are only expressions by the mind and the body of the spiritual principle that has been chosen. The ideal arises from the spiritual forces. Attitudes and activities can be ideals *only* to the extent that they express the conscious spirit in which we choose to live our lives.

For know first, the image must be in the spiritual ideal before it may become a factor in the mental self for material expression.   1440-2

. . .ideals are not your mind—ideals are principles acted upon *by* the mind.   2533-6

Physical Ideals

In the same way that the mental ideal is related to attitudes, the physical ideal is concerned with actions. We decide how we are going to give physical expression to the spiritual ideal in the areas of our lives with which we are willing to work. We ask ourselves, "What can I *do* in this area of my life that will bring into manifestation the same feeling or spirit that comes forth when I say the one word that I have chosen as my spiritual ideal?" Here we are concerned with specific actions, such as washing dishes, writing letters, or saying "thank you."

Physical *goals* are those things we desire as our material conditions—the kind of house, automobile or job that we want. Physical *ideals* are concerned with application and behavioral manifestation of the motivating spirit with respect to specific people and conditions. A physical ideal might be to keep a clean house, to drive safely, or to get our reports in on time at our job.

. . .the ideal material. . .Not of conditions, but what has brought, what does bring into manifestation the spiritual and mental ideals. What relationships does such bring to things, to individuals, to situations?   5091-3

We may say, "I have an ideal to meditate daily." What is the purpose for doing this? Is it to be more healthy or to develop ESP, or is this an activity which expresses an ideal that has arisen from the spirit within? If, for example, we choose the word "service" as the spiritual ideal, it is quite possible that daily meditation would result in a more healthy body capable of giving to others more effectively. Often we set standards which should more properly be called goals than ideals, because their purpose cannot be traced to a motivation concerned with the spirit behind the activity.

A Model for Writing Down Ideals

One of the most effective ways to write down ideals is to use a diagram consisting of three concentric circles. The inner circle will contain the one word which we choose as an expression of our spiritual ideal. As an example, suppose we choose the word *love*. The middle circle relates to the mental ideal or attitudes; the outer circle, to the physical ideal or actions.

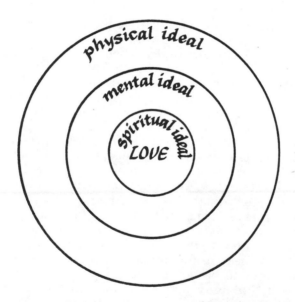

Next we divide the circles into pie-shaped segments, one for each area of our life selected for improvement. Suppose we select four (although we may want to deal with more than this): the relationship to ourself, to our spouse, to our job and to our next-door neighbor. Each segment is then labeled with the appropriate title.

In choosing the mental ideal toward ourselves, we may realize that the word "love" awakens in us the attitude toward ourselves that Jesus expressed when He said, "Neither do I condemn thee." We would then write the words "no selfcondemnation" in the appropriate section of the diagram. Being convinced that there is no condemnation and that it is only we who limit ourselves, we can consistently work with this attitude when self-condemning thoughts arise.

Now how are we going to give physical expression to this attitude? Perhaps it will come as a decision to be about the work that is at hand. Many times we look for reasons to disqualify ourselves. It is tempting to collect experiences and to say, "Now that I have gone through this—a broken marriage or some kind of surgery—I have sufficient excuse not to go ahead with life." If we work with forgiving ourselves, then we are less inclined to make excuses about why we can't be successful and more inclined to go ahead and apply and succeed in those things we know we ought to be doing. For most of us these physical applications that may bring the mental and spiritual into manifestation will include dietary changes, certain regular times of prayer and meditation, the discipline of dream study, and proper amounts of physical exercise.

In relationship to our spouse, we may decide that the *attitudes* of thoughtfulness and appreciativeness are awakened in us by the spiritual ideal of love. These attitudes can find physical expression as we make the effort to help wash the dishes each night or as we make saying "thank you" and being truly appreciative a daily experience.

In this hypothetical example we would then complete our ideals sheet using this same method to specify mental and physical ideals for the remaining two segments. It might be a good idea to do this in pencil and thus encourage ourselves to change aspects of our ideals as we find it necessary.

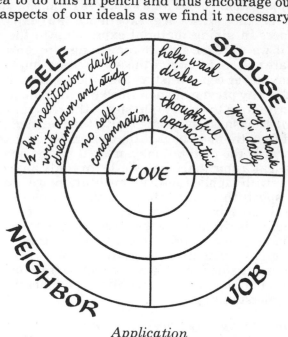

Application

The Edgar Cayce readings stress that to set an ideal and then to make no effort to become one with it only accentuates an awareness of separation. The Christ pattern is one of integration, not division. Setting a direction for growth without making some movement in that direction serves only to increase a sense of fragmentation within ourselves. Jesus expressed this principle in His teaching, "No man, having put his hand to the plow, and looking back, is fit for the kingdom of God." (Luke 9:62) If we set our sights upon a new orientation and the work it will entail, and then look back to the old ways and fail to do the work of application at hand, we make it much more difficult to grow into a higher state of consciousness.

In a sense, a statement of direction does not become an ideal without serious self-involvement. Such involvement is attained only by direct experience. In the experiencing and the application of the motivational spirit we wish to express, it becomes not just a theory of the mind, but an ideal.

103

For as ye apply them they become thy ideals. To be just as theories they do not belong to thee, they are still theories so far as thy personal being is concerned. It's the application of same that counts. What do they bring into thine experience? These are well if ye will apply them. 5091-3

In the application comes an awareness commensurate with the spirit of the ideal. We experience an expansion of consciousness in giving material expression to the ideal we have set. If we wait for a dramatic change in consciousness before we are willing to change the way we respond to life, that change may never come. Just as the process of writing down ideals in the way previously described is a movement from the center (spiritual) to the outer (physical), the *realization* of that state of consciousness associated with the spiritual ideal is a movement from the outer back to the center. We can move in our desires towards the motivation expressed by the one word we have chosen as a spiritual ideal. We do this only as we combine meditation with application: in meditation we awaken an authentic spirit; then in application the awareness expands and we feel more truly loving. The attainment of spiritual understanding is, in fact, the best criterion that man has by which to judge the direction he has chosen for his life. If his choice is founded upon material desires, it can at best lead only to a state of satisfaction. When the motivating force behind that direction is from the spirit within, the application leads to spiritual understanding.

Q-5. In what way may I best attain my ideal?
A-5. Well that an individual know that in the *attaining* of an ideal of an earthly making is satisfaction, and if of spiritual making is obtained only in *spiritual* understanding—which gives contentment. 262-13

One of the most important, as well as challenging, ways in which we can learn to apply our ideals is to look for the ways in which *others* manifest them. This is so integral a part of our growth process that the affirmation in the chapter of *A Search for God* entitled "What Is My Ideal?" ends with these words: "Let me see in my brother, that I see in Him whom I worship." (262-11) What is this but a recognition and acknowledgement of the fact that there is a oneness of spirit among all men?

As students of the Edgar Cayce readings, we often say, "The weaknesses we see in others are our own worst faults." Rarely do we express the corollary to this: "When we see the good in another, it is because that same goodness is in us." Both are expressions of a principle about the mind; let us keep in mind the affirmative way of stating this principle. Seeing another person express the spirit of the highest that we know awakens us to the bond that joins all mankind.

Then little by little, line by line, may the body-consciousness become conscious of the Spirit of the Master working in and through the acts, the thoughts, the *life* of the body. *See* in each individual that they represent of the ideal set by self, and live the life, the whole concept, of thine own ideal.   262-11

Know that [which] thou would worship, and self a part of same, seeing in others then that thou would worship in the Father; for the prayer was, "May they be one, even as Thou and I are one," for as given, a *spiritual insight* brings the *seeing* of the best in each life. There is good in all, for they *are* of the Father, and have been bought with the price, even of the Son, in that flesh may know the *glory* of the Father that may be manifested even in thee!   262-12

Ideals and Affirmations

After we have written down our ideals and have begun to work at applying them, times may arise when we feel out of touch with the spirit by which we have chosen to direct our lives. We may need a way to return from our state of depression, indolence or self-condemnation. We need a place where we can go in consciousness and start out again. By choosing affirmations relevant to our ideals we can re-orient ourselves.

Certainly there is a place for working with a specific affirmation in our daily meditations. There is also a place for using an affirmation in our work with specific persons and conditions. For each area of our life that we have specified in writing down our ideals, we can write an affirmation that will help us attain the ideal attitude towards that particular relationship. The affirmation is a statement that allows us to maintain the kind of attitude that would grow out of what we have set for ourselves as a spiritual ideal. From the earlier example, if we feel that we need an affirmation regarding our spouse, it might be: "Father God, awaken thoughtfulness and appreciation within me that I might be a more loving servant to others." When we feel ourselves becoming angry or hurt, we can say the affirmation as an aid in helping us return to our center. If we are working to replace a self-condemning attitude, as indicated in the earlier example, there is an exceptionally beneficial affirmation given in the readings:

. . . not how I faltered, but did I seek His face again? 281-7

Every time we are about to move into a self-condemning thought we may catch ourselves with this affirmation and turn about and face the Light.

The replacement of a negative thought with a positive one is a sound procedure both psychologically and spiritually. We replace the doubt or confusion with a new attitude expressed by the affirmation. In writing these affirmations for the various aspects of our lives, not only do we specify a direction in which we want to face, a new attitude, but we also provide a guideline for orienting ourselves toward it.

This practice can be illustrated by the way in which Jesus met temptation in the wilderness. As He became aware of His great psychic ability, it occurred to Him, "There are several ways I can go about this work. For one, I could be a psychic and perform miracles." Thus we have the story that the devil came to Him and said, "Why don't you turn this stone into bread." He replied, in essence, "I have a place to stand. I have set my purpose; I have something to return to now that I face a decision. It has been written (not just in Scripture, but within my mind as an ideal), 'Man does not live by bread alone.' I will not make my decision based upon the need that man has for bread, because man has other needs." It should be clear to us that Jesus met temptation not by just quoting Scripture, but rather by evaluating the impulse in comparison to a high standard of motivation. Even so, there is a very close parallel between this special use of affirmation and Scripture reading. Every student on the path needs a "scripture," a literature which awakens "mantrically," as it were, a renewed sense of purpose and rededication. The fact that Edgar Cayce read the Bible so regularly may be the real key to his steadfast attunement and thus his helpfulness to others.

We can meet every temptation that faces us by returning to an affirmation that corresponds to an ideal. When we are tempted by a negative attitude we need to have something to put in its place. We do not just stop doing what is wrong—we start doing something that is right. Jesus told about cleaning out an evil spirit but having nothing with which to replace it. The original evil spirit will return with seven more, and the second state of the man will be worse than the first. This parable stresses the replacement principle, which the readings describe with the words "supersede" and "supplant."

Because of past experiences, each of us has certain predisposed sets or tendencies which make us likely to respond in particular ways. As we work at the conscious level, using our free will, we may choose the patterns by which we want to anchor our responses. We must be prepared to replace all our negative unconscious predispositions with constructive

106

purposes. This is a way of understanding how we deal with karma. One reading asks, "What is karma but giving way to impulse?" (622-6) Another says that the subconscious mind "...may be best classified, in the physical sense, as a habit." (262-10) Because these impulses or habits reside within us, predisposing us, we must decide in advance upon alternative responses. We do this by choosing an ideal and then specifying for ourselves mental attitudes that we think would grow out of that ideal. We work with an affirmation that will enable us to return to the attitude that we think is optimum with regard to those areas of our lives. This is the process for awakening the consciousness of the Christ that is within: set a spiritual ideal, meditate and dwell upon that which we wish to become, and work at the application of that ideal as it finds expression in our attitudes and actions. Thus, when periods of temptation or confusion arise, we have established a pattern for returning to a stable place to stand.

The Psalmist wrote:

> God is our refuge and strength, a very present help in trouble.
> Therefore will not we fear, though the earth be removed, and though the mountains be carried into the midst of the sea . . .
> There is a river, the streams whereof shall make glad the city of God, the holy place of the tabernacles of the most High . . .
> Be still, and know that I am God . . . (Ps. 46, KJV)

> Blessed is the man . . . [whose] delight is in the law of the Lord; and in his law doth he meditate day and night. And he shall be like a tree planted by the rivers of water, that bringeth forth his fruit in his season; his leaf also shall not wither; and whatsoever he doeth shall prosper. (Ps. 1, KJV)

Nearly all the principles presented in this text are incorporated in the following reading; thus it constitutes an excellent summary. The information given is applicable, reassuring, inspirational, and philosophically profound.

[Edgar Cayce's reading given on October 8, 1941, for a 62-year-old woman writer, Protestant:]

In giving a mental and spiritual reading for this body, we find that there needs to be only those suggestions as may remind the body of the abilities of the mind to make those mental and spiritual applications—in its own self—that may enable the body to keep that attunement to the Creative Forces, which is the birthright of each and every soul.

For this entity, then, the premises from which such advice or counsel may be obtained should be well understood or comprehended—as to the sources:

One finds the body, the mind, the soul of self as a counterpart of that an entity worships in the Godhead as Father, Son and Holy Spirit.

So the body, mind and soul answer to that which is the source of health, of mind, of matter, in the experience of each entity.

To this entity these in the Godhead are one. So in the body, they are one; body, mind, soul.

Body is temporal, mind is partially temporal and partially holy; the soul is eternal.

Just as the body then is the manifestation of the individual entity, the mind is the manifestation of the Son—both as an earthly experience and as an at-onement with the Father, the Whole.

So the soul is that which is eternal.

Thus does there come in the experience of each soul those problems in a material world of the constant warring of material or changing things, or earthly experience, with mental and spiritual or soul forces.

The *Way,* then, is that manifested in the Creative Force through Jesus, the Christ, the Son; for He is the way, the truth, the light in which the body, the mind, the soul may find that security, that understanding, that comprehending of the oneness *of* the spiritual with the material that is manifested in an individual entity.

To this entity, problems arise in the body-forces. While the mind is in attune, the soul is in at-onement, the physical conditions to the entity become as stumbling blocks.

Remember rather the pattern as was manifested for thee in the Son; how that though He were the Son, yet learned He obedience through the things which He suffered.

He used, then, that which was necessary in the experience in the earth as periods of suffering, as periods of rejection, even by His own that He had called, that were His friends; not as stumbling stones but as stepping-stones to make for thee, for the world, that access for each soul, for the closer relationship of the Father through the Son, to the children of men.

This is thy heritage, then; not as one that knows not, but as one being reminded—put on the whole armor. Fret not at those things that may appear to hinder, but to let that harmony as thou has expressed, as thou may express to others, be in such measures as to bring—even as He—that hope, that light, that peace which comes from the closer walk with Him day by day.

Let thy prayer be, ever, *"Here am I, Lord: use me, in that way, in that manner Thou seest fit: not my will but Thine, O God, be done in me, through me, day by day. May my going in, my coming out, be always acceptable in Thy sight."*

Then use thy abilities in thy writing, in thy meditation, in thy composition, to tell the glory of the oneness of the Christ as may be manifested in body, in mind, in soul.

And as this awakens those influences in others, so does it bring to thee that peace, that harmony, that understanding that makes the closer walk with Him.

Remember, as He gave, "If ye love me, keep my commandments. My commandments are not grievous, only that ye love one another, even as I have loved thee."

Then as we keep such in our daily conversation, in our daily dealings with our fellow man, in that same manner as we think toward or treat our fellow man, so we do unto the Lord our God, so we do unto our Savior, our Brother—who gave *all* that we might know that onement with the body, mind, soul in Him.

For He *is* the way, the truth. They that approach any other way become those that cheat themselves, robbing themselves of the truth that would bring the preventing of those things that separate man from the love of the Father.

As to thy service, as to thy light unto others:

Who may tell the rose how to be beautiful? Who may tell the stars or the moon in its course how to raise in the heart and soul of man the longing to know the Creator of all?

And remember, as has been given, in Him is all. There was nothing made that was made that was not made by Him—the way, the truth, the light.

Then, let not thy heart be troubled; ye believe in God, believe in Him also, who has promised to come and walk with thee, yea, to talk with thee, as ye seek to know His biddings.

Ready for questions.

Q-1. Was there a spiritual and psychic cause for my breakdown in 1929 as well as a physical one?

A-1. Doubt brought the psychic experience, with the physical weakness.

Do not count these as weaknesses, for remember, the weakness of man may become the strength of God—in and through man using same as a channel through which others may be brought to know of the light, of the love of the Father for the children of men.

Q-2. What has caused the abnormal fears from which I suffered?

A-2. Doubt!

Let not thy heart be troubled, neither let it be afraid. Cling closer—call until He answers. For the promise has ever been—

"Though ye may be far, if ye will call—believing—I will *hear,* and answer *speedily."*

Read again, and again, the 14th, 15th, 16th and 17th of John; not merely as rote, but as though ye—as an individual—were speaking to thy Lord, thy Master, thy Brother. And ye will find the answer, ye will find that doubt and fear—and those things that may have troubled thee—will flee away; and there will come that peace as is promised. Know that He is able to keep that He hath promised. For He overcame death, hell and the grave, and is the God of the *living*—not of the dead nor of the past! For all is the present, *now,* in Him. As the Father, the Son and the Holy Ghost are one, so are the body, mind and soul one. Hold them; hold that as a fact, as an understanding; and ye will find peace . . .

Q-6. How can I obtain relief from resentment and bitterness?

A-6. As ye forgive, ye are forgiven. As ye love, so are ye loved. As ye resent, so are ye resented. This is *law,* physical, mental and *spiritual!*

Then, chuck it out of thy life. Let the love of God so fill thy mind, thy body, that there is *no* resentment.

As to how—though ye may not of thyself, put the burden on Him and it becomes light. But *act* in the manner as He did, not resenting any. For remember, as He said to that one who had promised that though all might forsake Him, he never would, yet in the same hour denied that he ever knew Him, "When thou art converted, strengthen thy brethren." Thus may it be given to thee, if ye put that resentment away, if ye put that doubt and that fear upon Him, He will cast it out; but thee, strengthen thy brethren. Teach, preach, talk to others, as to how they should leave such at the Cross and *only* magnify, manifest, *know* that they need not attempt to justify themselves. For, *all* the justification is in Him. We need then only to *glorify* that love, that hope, that understanding which He brings to each soul that seeks His face.   2600-2

Coda

We are children of God, made in His image, miniature replicas of the universe, containing within us in our present finite state a pattern of wholeness. When we choose that pattern as the ideal, the motivational criterion of our lives, when we awaken it with the imaginative forces of the mind and nurture it in daily meditation and application, we begin to become that pattern. The Spirit begins to flow through us because the Spirit of love has an affinity for the pattern of love. We begin to fulfill that for which we were created and for which we are destined: to be conformed to the image of His Son.

110

Chapter Seven

A SYSTEMATIC APPROACH

A sound understanding of the theoretical bases of meditation should be helpful; however, *the important thing is that we meditate,* consistently, persistently, joyfully and confidently. The following step-by-step procedure, based on the Edgar Cayce readings, is presented to give a sense of confidence regarding how to meditate properly.

In evaluating a meditation procedure, two things should be kept in mind. First, the source of the readings stressed the relativity of individual points of view. Even in the near-claim that this approach is according to that presented by the Master, the readings said this is *a* way, not *the* way, to meditate. Second, no matter how strongly they recommended persistency and consistency, the readings discouraged doing things by rote. Whether in relation to exercise, diet, or castor oil packs, they encouraged making changes in the routine. An implication of these insights from the readings is that we should avoid a sense of ritual in meditation, if being ritualists means that we feel there is only one proper way and we must do it that way every time.

Nevertheless, there are many people who benefit from following specific guidelines, and there are many important principles involved in proper meditation, which are incorporated in the following procedure. Therefore we encourage you to *try* this approach in every detail. Later you may deviate from it as you find good reasons for doing so, and as you find variations which bring new life and joy into your meditation. A major way in which to *grow* in meditation is to use the growth sequence of affirmations, concepts and application disciplines found in the *Search for God* materials.

From the Edgar Cayce readings we can outline definite steps to be taken as an approach to meditation. Check the appropriate space as you complete each item and feel that you understand it.

111

1. *Affirm these fundamental premises about the nature of man.*
   ( ) A. "Hear, O Israel, the Lord thy God is One" means that there is only one force or energy in the universe. All that exists is, at its deepest level, a part of this fundamental oneness.
   ( ) B. In his experience in the earth, man lives in a three-dimensional state of consciousness. Because of this, he finds it helpful to work with threefold concepts. He conceives of the Godhead as a Trinity—Father, Son, and Holy Spirit—and of himself in a corresponding way—body, mind, and soul.
   ( ) C. Since the three aspects of man are linked by an underlying unity, anything that affects one will affect the other two. Thus, in approaching meditation we must consider physical, mental, and spiritual factors.
   ( ) D. Our nature is basically spiritual or divine, and we are all capable of attuning ourselves to it. The answer to our desire for wholeness and love is found in God. We meet Him within the temple of our own being.
   ( ) E. The consciousness in which one finds himself is only one of countless possible states of awareness.
   ( ) F. There is one state of consciousness which is in perfect accord with the nature of the spirit within: the consciousness of the Christ. It is described in the readings as "the awareness within each soul, imprinted in pattern on the mind and waiting to be awakened by the will, of the soul's oneness with God." (5749-14) It is a state of awareness of the oneness of God with all creation. It is a potential that already exists within us at an unconscious level and which can be brought into awareness as we exercise our will to awaken it.
   ( ) G. Meditation is the most effective way to awaken this pattern and to invite contact with God within ourselves. The realization that we can meet the Spirit of God within ourselves is the most fundamental principle of meditation, and for this reason it has been referred to as "the secret of secrets."
   ( ) H. After thinking through and rationally analyzing these statements, take time to contemplate and reflect upon the meaning of each one. Spend five to ten minutes of quiet time on each statement, getting a feeling for its essence.

2. *Formulate a clear definition of meditation.*
( ) A. Study the following definitions from the readings.
   Meditation is listening to the Divine within.
   1861-19

   This emphasizes the fact that meditation is a receptive or listening state. It is the practice of stillness and quietness. In this case the word "listening" means an attentiveness to the deepest inner processes.

   (2) **[Meditation] is not musing, not daydreaming; but, as ye find your bodies made up of the physical, mental and spiritual, it is the attuning of the mental body and the physical body to its spiritual source.** 281-41

   This refers to the fact that meditation is a process that involves all three aspects of man: body, mind, and soul. If there is to be an alignment within ourselves—if we are to experience a state of integration and wholeness—it can only be as the changeable parts of ourselves (body and mind) come into accord with the unchangeable (the spiritual forces of the soul). To let the mind wander and daydream is to give attention to thought patterns within the mind that are less than one's ideal, and this is *not* deep meditation. There is no end to the images that we can entertain as they arise from the unconscious. We must not make the mistake of believing that "the mind" means only the conscious mind, and that anything that arises from the unconscious is therefore of the Spirit. There is a whole realm of thought patterns in the unconscious which are of a limiting or illusory nature. We have created them and they are very likely to break forth into consciousness as we begin to be still. They may be expressed as an attitude or thought that comes to mind, as a visual form, or as a disturbance in the physical body. Undoubtedly, many of these will create fascinating and captivating experiences, but to stop at this point and give attention to them is not deep meditation.

   (3) *Meditation* is *emptying* self of all that hinders the creative forces from rising along the natural channels of the physical man to be disseminated through those centers and sources that create

the activities of the physical, the mental, the spiritual man; properly done must make one *stronger* mentally, physically ...   281-13

Our relationship to limiting thought patterns is referred to in the phrase *"emptying* self of all that hinders ... " Until we move beyond selfish and unloving patterns within us (both physical and mental), they stand as a barrier between the conscious mind and the consciousness of the Christ. In meditation we are letting go of our involvement with those things that bring on such attitudes as confusion, self-pity, and frustration. By turning our attention away from anything that is less than the truth of our own inner being, we move into the stillness of meditation. It is significant to note that the above reading uses the word "natural." The physical body is particularly suited for the process of meditation. It is important that we understand this fact and define meditation for ourselves as an activity that is a natural and indispensable step in our spiritual unfoldment in the earth.

( ) B. Differentiate in your own mind between prayer and meditation. The readings emphasize that prayer is an *activity* of the conscious mind:

   ... the concerted effort of the physical consciousness to become attuned to the consciousness of the Creator ...   281-13

( ) C. Write your own definition of meditation, incorporating those concepts from the above definitions that are personally meaningful to you. (Use the space below.)

3. *Set your ideals and purposes.*
   ( ) A. Consider these principles:
      (1) Meditation is more than an action; it encompasses an entire approach to life. It is misleading to suggest that one practice a technique of meditation without first considering the ideals and purposes for doing it.
      (2) There is always a "why" of meditation assumed along with the "how." It is better to make this assumption explicit. To determine this we must ask ourselves, "Why do I want to meditate?"

(3) Success in meditation will not exceed the ideal that we set for ourselves.

(4) Meditation is an effective way to awaken a wide variety of possible experiences (including the development of psychic ability, the remembrance of past lives, the movement of powerful energy currents through the body, etc.).

(5) It is important to remember that our desire for specific experiences to be awakened in meditation is no guarantee that they will lead to God.

(6) There should be only one purpose for meditation: to attune ourselves to God. Any other purpose or ideal is likely to lead us astray as we work with meditation.

(7) We may find that as we continue to meditate we become more psychic, our bodies become more healthy, or certain experiences occur; but these are to be accepted as natural side effects of meditation and not as the purpose.

( ) B. Write down what you have set for yourself as a spiritual ideal. You may want to write just one word that represents the highest spiritual quality that you know, or you may prefer to write out this ideal in a longer form.

( ) C. Write down the ideal mental attitudes that you have set for yourself. What attitudes would you manifest if your life were being totally directed by your spiritual ideal? Try to think of these in terms of the relationships that you have in your life (e.g., "I have an ideal mental attitude of *patience* in my relationship with my son," or, "I have an ideal mental attitude of *persistence* in my job.").

( ) D. Write down the physical ideals that you have set for yourself. These should be specific activities that would express your spiritual and mental ideals (e.g., "I am going to write down my dreams each morning," or, "I am going to help my wife with housecleaning every weekend.").

( ) E. Explain how meditation can be an expression of your ideals.

4. *Understand the role of the physical body in meditation.*
    ( ) A. Consider these principles:
    (1) Our work in the material world is to bring the attributes of the spiritual life *into* the physical.
    (2) We overcome the three-dimensional, material world and move beyond it as we bring the

consciousness of love into our material existence.

(3) God has promised to meet us face to face within the temple, which is the physical body.

(4) Our bodies are constructed in such a way that spiritual awakening can be a natural process.

(5) There are spiritual centers or contact points within the body that are directly related to the process of meditation.

( ) B. Read *Meditation—Gateway to Light,* by Elsie Sechrist (particularly chapters 3, 4 and 5). It offers a detailed description of the spiritual centers.

( ) C. Read the section entitled "Meditation" in *Venture Inward,* by Hugh Lynn Cayce.

5. *Understand the importance of the mind to meditation.*

( ) A. Consider these principles:

(1) The statement "Mind is the builder" is especially true for meditation.

(2) As the life force is awakened in meditation, particular patterns within the unconscious mind are activated (i.e., memory patterns).

(3) That held mentally during meditation determines which patterns will be activated.

(4) Our growth (or lack of growth) in awareness is directly affected by those memory patterns which are awakened.

(5) It is better to choose consciously a direction for growth than to permit memories to be awakened randomly or haphazardly in meditation.

(6) A statement of your ideal or an "affirmation" serves as an effective focal point for your attention during meditation. (The use of the affirmation will be covered at a later point.)

In completing the steps outlined up to this point, we have set the foundation necessary for effective meditation as it is described in the readings. The next steps concern procedures that are employed before or during *each meditation period.* We must keep in mind the fact that, in living the spiritual life, our concern with the *attitude* in which an action is carried out supersedes the importance of any technique. We must never let the *form* we use so control us that we forget the purpose of meditation. Nevertheless, we cannot reject form, because we are seeking to give form or expression to the Spirit.

6. *Decide upon a suitable time, place and position for meditation.*

( ) A. Read the following story and try to relate the principle concerning time to your own experience.

A man took a new job which required him to be at work at 8:30 a.m. Therefore, on Sunday night he set his alarm clock to awaken him at seven o'clock the next morning. He continued this practice for the rest of the week, but on Friday night he went to bed intending to sleep late the next morning. However, on Saturday morning he awakened at seven o'clock, just as he did the previous mornings, this time without the alarm clock.

( ) B. Consider the following principles concerning the time of day for meditation.

    (1) We should meditate at the time we are most likely to be capable of attuning ourselves to our ideal.

    (2) For all people, the period from 2:00 to 3:00 in the morning is particularly suited for meditation. Since activity levels in the world around us will be at a low point, we can make good use of this period of minimal psychic and physical noise if we have slept several hours beforehand. Do you feel that you can make a realistic commitment at this time in your life to meditate at some time between 2:00 and 3:00 a.m.?
        _____ yes   _____ no

    (3) A second period of time in which many people find a helpful environmental influence is just before or at sunrise. Do you feel that you can make a realistic commitment at this time in your life to meditate then?
        _____ yes   _____ no

    (4) Think about each of the following factors in your life and how they each help you select the best time of day for meditation.
        (a) Daily schedule.
        (b) Bodily rhythms (e.g., low-energy times of the day might be unsuitable).
        (c) The amount of devotion and commitment you feel for meditation.

( ) C. Select a specific time (or times) at which you intend to meditate each day. (Write it down here:) _____
If you find that the time you select does not work well for you, review this section of the manual and make another choice of time.

( ) D. Decide the amount of time that you will spend on each meditation session.
    (1) If you are just beginning to meditate, it is best to

choose shorter periods of time (e.g., 10 to 15 minutes).

(2) There should be some degree of consistency in the length of meditations. For example, half an hour daily is preferable to a schedule consisting of hour-long meditations twice a week and ten-minute periods on the other days.

(3) Remember that it is *attunement* that we seek, not just the logging of a certain amount of time. One moment in the presence of the Christ is worth far more than half an hour, or a thousand years, spent daydreaming and calling it meditation.

(4) How important is your spiritual search to you? Can you give your undivided attention to your spiritual ideal in meditation with the same regularity and enthusiasm that you give to television programs or your favorite hobbies?

(5) Specify the approximate amount of time that you will spend on each meditation session. (Write that number here:) _____ minutes.

( ) E. Select a particular place where you will meditate daily. It is best to choose a place where you are unlikely to be interrupted. (Write that place here:)

_____

( ) F. Choose a position for meditation after considering these points:

(1) One should be comfortable in order to minimize bodily distractions.

(2) The spine should be straight.

(3) Choose a position in which you are not likely to fall asleep.

(4) Those who choose a supine position are encouraged to fold their hands over the area of the solar plexus.

(5) Those who have no particular preference for a position will probably find that the following one will work for them:

Sit up straight in a chair with feet flat on the floor and the hands either folded in the lap or placed on top of the thighs.

(6) Indicate the position you will use:

( ) supine (with hands over the solar plexus)
( ) cross-legged (the lotus position)
( ) sitting in a chair or on a couch
( ) other (describe) _____

7. *Do those preparatory activities that are personally helpful.*
( ) A. Review principles concerning the purpose of preparation:
   (1) In meditation we are dealing with a powerful energy.
   (2) Impurities (both mental and physical) which can be removed by conscious effort should be eliminated before meditation. Otherwise, they will only be magnified by the meditation process.
   (3) Preparation consists of not only the things we do in the short amount of time before meditation; it also includes everything we do in our daily lives. We are constantly preparing for our next meditation.
( ) B. Specify short-term preparations that you will use (indicate the appropriate ones).
   (1) Cleansing the body:
       [ ] (a) Take a shower or bath.
       [ ] (b) Wash specific parts of the body.
       [ ] (c) Drink a glass of water.
       [ ] (d) Other (list) _____.
   (2) Abstaining from certain activities for a specific amount of time prior to meditation (e.g., no smoking within an hour of beginning meditation, no eating within two hours, etc.):
       Activity (list)   Time between activity and meditation

( ) C. Specify ongoing preparations that you will make.
   (1) List those attitudes and emotions you wish to transform:

   (2) List those attitudes and emotions you wish to manifest more frequently:

( ) D. Work towards having a more balanced diet.
   (1) We have all experienced ways in which our eating habits affect our state of consciousness. Many people find it difficult to stay awake after a big dinner; others are irritable or depressed if they skip breakfast. Any consideration of changing one's state of awareness should include the maximum that "you are what you eat." Certainly, nutritional factors are only a part of the influences that shape us, but they are very important ones.

119

(2) It is possible to become so fanatical about the purity of food that we forget the true purpose for attuning the body: to express love in the earth. A sense of balance is needed. We should change those things that we can and provide our bodies with the nourishment required to function properly.

(3) Consider the following dietary recommendations from the readings. Decide upon the degree to which you intend to plan your diet according to each recommendation (e.g., I am going to cut down to eating beef only twice a week).

(a) Eliminate all meats except fish, fowl, and lamb.

(b) Eat very few cakes and pastries (or other starches combined with sweets).

(c) Eliminate overly refined or processed foods.

(d) Avoid fruits and vegetables (especially tomatoes) that are picked before ripening on the vine.

(e) Avoid the combination of milk and citrus fruits.

(f) Avoid the combination of whole-grain cereals and citrus fruit.

(g) Avoid the combination of coffee and milk or cream.

(h) Eliminate the combination of starches and proteins.

(i) Eat 80% alkaline-producing foods (e.g., most fruits and vegetables) and 20% acid-producing foods (e.g., meats, cereals and starches).

(j) Eat three vegetables that grow above the ground for every one that grows below (e.g., spinach, corn and tomatoes with carrots).

(Refer to *The Normal Diet* for answers to any questions you may have. This booklet is available from the A.R.E. Press.)

8. *Employ those aids for attunement which you find helpful.*
( ) A. Consider the following points before choosing the techniques you want to use before each meditation.

(1) Techniques to enhance attunement are an individual matter. That which is helpful to one person may be distracting to another.

(2) Any procedure or technique we choose is only a means, not an end.

120

(3) If one feels unable to meditate because he has run out of his favorite incense or because he cannot do a particular chant, he has missed the point of meditation.
(4) Study the following reading, which differentiates between that which aids attunement and that to which we seek to be attuned.

> *Q-2. How can I use the astronomical, the numerical, the environs of the creations in the vibrations from metal, from stones, which influence me, to advantage in my present life?*
> **A-2. As these are but lights, but signs in thine experience, they are as but a candle that one stumbles not in the dark. But worship *not* the light of the candle; rather that to which it may guide thee in thy service. So, whether from the vibrations of numbers, of metals, of stones, these are merely to become the necessary influences to make thee in attune, one with the Creative Forces; just as the pitch of a song of praise is not the song or the message therein, but is a helpmeet for those that would find strength in the service of the Lord. So, use them to attune self. How, ye ask? As ye apply, ye are given the next step.** 707-2

( ) B. Music
(1) What experiences have you had in which sound affected both physical processes and consciousness (e.g., you may have found that college fight songs induce adrenal activity and the accompanying sense of excitement)? Write an example here:

(2) Properly selected music can help one get still for meditation. Remember that the music should be turned off once it has done this job and is not to be left on during the entire meditation.
(3) Do you feel that music would be helpful, and do you intend to use it? ____ yes ____ no
(4) If "yes," what specific musical selection(s) do you intend to use at the beginning of your meditation period?

( ) C. Chants
(1) The readings relate particular sounds to the opening or the awakening of the spiritual centers. These sounds can be used in chants.

(2) Two simple chants that you might want to use are "aum" (sometimes spelled "om") and "ah-re-aum" (or "ah-re-om").

(3) Recommendations to those who wish to work with chanting:

   (a) The chant is usually repeated aloud three or seven times.

   (b) The length of each repetition is usually five to fifteen seconds.

   (c) One should breathe deeply before each repetition and intone the chant on a note that is comfortable for his voice. If you are using a multisyllabic chant (e.g, "ah-re-aum"), breathe only at the beginning of each repetition, not between the syllables.

   (d) The effectiveness of chants is not determined by the loudness. Some people mistakenly believe that if they chant twice as loud, they will derive twice as much benefit. Often, however, this practice only disperses energy. The chant can be so soft that another person, even in the same room, may hardly hear you.

   (e) Chanting is effective only if it is coupled with an understanding that the true purpose for meditation is to attune ourselves to God.

   The tone, then—find it in thyself, if ye would be enlightened. To give the tune or tone as Do, Ah—aum—would mean little; unless there is the comprehending, the understanding of that to which ye are attempting to attune—in the spiritual, the mental, the material.   2072-10

   (If you are interested in chants, read chapter 6 of the book *Music as the Bridge,* by Shirley Winston.)

(4) Do you intend to chant at the beginning of meditation?

          _____ yes   _____ no

( ) D. Incense

   (1) For some people the olfactory system is particularly sensitive to influences which can aid attunement. You may want to try using some incense during meditation to see if it is helpful.

   (2) Consider this passage from a reading given for an individual who was told that use of incense would be beneficial.

For this body—not for everybody—odors would have much to do with the ability of the entity to meditate. For the entity in the experiences through the Temple of Sacrifice became greatly attuned through the sense of smell . . . "feel" the essence of the incense through the body-forces in its motion of body. This will open the kundaline forces of the body. Then direct same to be a blessing to others. **2823-3**

    (3) Check the appropriate space when you have decided whether or not to use incense.

               _____ yes   _____ no

( ) E. Reading inspirational material

    (1) Some people find that reading from the Bible or some other inspirational book for a brief period of time is a very helpful activity.

    (2) Do you feel that it would be beneficial for you to do this just before meditation? _____ yes _____ no

    (3) If "yes," list some of those things that you might read.

( ) F. Exercises

    (1) Anything that brings vitality and balance to the physical body will aid meditation. What specific types and amounts of exercise do you intend to do daily in order to help your meditations (e.g., 15 minutes of yoga before breakfast)?

    (2) The readings describe a head-and-neck exercise that many have found beneficial just before meditation. The procedure can be described as follows:

Sit upright with the spine straight. Drop your head forward slowly and raise it back up. Complete this movement three times. Let your head drop *back* slowly and raise it back up three times. Then do the same movement three times to the right and to the left. Finally, let your head drop forward and rotate it three times in a clockwise direction and three times counterclockwise. Allow your head to extend downward, to the sides and backward as far as it will go without pain or discomfort. Do you intend to use this exercise? _____ yes _____ no

    (3) The readings, as well as many other sources, refer to the close relationship between the breath and consciousness. The following breathing exercise

was recommended for use before meditation: Cover the left nostril. Breathe in slowly and deeply through the right nostril, and exhale through the mouth. Do this three times. Next cover the right nostril and inhale through the left, then cover the left nostril and exhale through the right. Do this three times. Do you intend to use this exercise? _____ yes _____ no

( ) G. Light and colors

Several people questioned Edgar Cayce about the use of lights and colors (such as an external light in the room or a color held in the mind) during meditation. Read the following passages given in answer to these questions.

Q-7. When meditating at night, what color light should I use?

A-7. White light. Any colored lights make for a diffusion of that as may be perfect. What light was in Him that is Light, that is Life, that is out of darkness? *White* light!   275-39

Q-2. Give color [that] this body might meditate upon beneficially for self-healing.

A-2. The white light of the Christ, if the body, in itself, would find help. It isn't the color, it isn't the vibration—it is rather the awareness of entering into the spirit of truth, the power of health, the power of love. Do that.   1861-11

( ) H. Prayer

(1) In prayer the conscious mind makes a concerted effort to be attuned to the chosen ideal. Having done this, it is much easier for the mind to achieve the heightened awareness of meditation.

(2) A prayer of protection has been written based upon a passage from reading 262-3:
"Father, as I open myself to the unseen forces that surround the throne of Grace and Beauty and Might, I throw about myself the protection that is found in the thought of the Christ."
This prayer should be used to help sense the protective presence of the Christ, not as a magic ritual. Do you feel that this prayer would be helpful, and do you intend to use it?
_____ yes   _____ no

(3) No prayer is more suited for aiding the attunement process of meditation than the Lord's Prayer. The readings indicate that Jesus taught this prayer to His disciples because its meaning may act to awaken the spiritual centers. For each of its parts, a relative correspondence may be assigned to the activity of one of the endocrine glands. (A description of this correspondence can be found on page 42.)

Do you intend to use the Lord's Prayer at the beginning of meditation?

_____ yes _____ no

You should now list those procedures that you will do daily as a part of your meditation period. Certain items below have been described as optional. Cross out those that you have chosen not to work with. Those which remain will constitute a step-by-step description of the beginning of your meditation session.

Abstain from particular activities for specified times.
Cleanse the body.
Arrive at designated meditation place at proper time.
Put on appropriate music for a brief time.
Light incense.
Read a passage from an inspirational book.
Do head-and-neck exercise.
Do breathing exercise.
Chant.
Prayer for protection.
Repeat the Lord's Prayer.

9. *Focus attention on an affirmation.*
( ) A. Consider the following points about the affirmation:
(1) Recall the principle "Mind is the builder." In meditation this is of particular importance because we are making an effort to build a new sense of identity based upon the awareness of our oneness with God. Unless the mind cooperates in this effort, there is little hope for success.
(2) There is considerable controversy among the various schools of thought concerning the way in which the mind should be used in meditation. Many agree that a quality of one-pointedness is necessary, so that the mind is not carried away by the endless array of images and thoughts that arise from the unconscious. Some suggest that one choose an object from the material world and

125

give it undivided attention (e.g., a rock, the flame of a candle, or a flower). Others recommend concentration upon a sound, color or image. While not specifically rejecting *any* technique, the Edgar Cayce readings say that in meditation the mind should be focused upon that which has been chosen as the spiritual ideal.

(3) For most people this is effectively done by using an expression of the ideal. Such an expression is a tool which serves as a reminder of the ideal. An affirmation can be used in this way.

(4) The readings suggest hundreds of affirmations, each consisting of a set of phrases or sentences expressing an ideal. Here are three examples from the Search for God readings:

Not my will but thine, O Lord, be done in and through me. Let me ever be a channel of blessings, today, now, to those that I contact, in *every* way. Let my going in, mine coming outs, be in accord with that *Thou* would have me do, and as the call comes, Here am I, send me—use me!

262-3

Father, as we seek to see and know Thy face, may we each—as individuals, and as a group—come to know ourselves, even as we are known, that we—as lights in Thee—may give the better concept of Thy Spirit in this world.

262-5

God be merciful to me! Help Thou my unbelief! Let me *see* in Him that Thou would have me see in my fellow man! Let me see in my brother that I see in that I worship!

262-11

(5) The Lord's Prayer can be used not only as an aid for attunement at the beginning of the meditation period, but also as an affirmation during the time of silence.

(6) Select an affirmation for your personal use.
   (a) If you are in a Search for God Study Group, continue to work with the affirmation for the chapter your group is currently studying.
   (b) If you are not working with a Study Group, you are encouraged to select one of the three affirmations given in #4 above.

(c) If you feel strongly that you need to use a different affirmation than those suggested, write it here:

(d) Read the chapter entitled "Meditation" in *A Search for God,* Book I. If you have read it before, read it again as a review.
( ) B. How to use the affirmation:
(1) Once you have selected the affirmation you intend to use, take time to study it. Look up any words that are not clear to you. Analyze it completely until you feel that you have arrived at the best intellectual understanding of this affirmation of which you are capable. Once you begin to use the affirmation in meditation it is important to resist any temptation to "figure it out." All work of this nature should be done beforehand. During this research period, write out your understanding of the ideas and meanings expressed in the affirmation that you will be using.
(2) We should be interested in the *meaning* or the *spirit* of the affirmation. The important thing is not so much the intellectual interpretation of the words, but the *response* that comes from within. An example of this principle can be found in the following answer to a question concerning the use of the Lord's Prayer:

As in feeling, as it were, the flow of the meanings of each portion of same throughout the body-physical. 281-29

What does the particular affirmation you have chosen awaken within you?
(3) When you have completed the various aids for attunement, you are ready for the period of silence in meditation. Begin by saying the affirmation to yourself (it may be helpful to do this more than once). Listen for a response from within yourself to the meaning or spirit of those words. It may come as a feeling (e.g., love, joy,

127

peace, well-being) or as a heightened state of awareness. Focus your attention on the spirit of that response.

(4) We must be careful not to expect overwhelming meditation experiences. It may be that one experiences only a slight change in feeling or in consciousness as a response to the affirmation. The important thing is to focus on *that* spirit, and not on other things that come to mind which create distractions.

(5) At some point you will very likely find that your mind drifts off. There is no end to the things that may come forth demanding attention. Some people notice bodily sensations; others remember an event from years before. No matter what form these distractions take, they should be dealt with in the same way:

(a) Have patience with yourself. Resist any temptation to condemn yourself for having drifted off.

(b) Repeat the affirmation (or a portion of it) and once again focus your attention on the inner response.

(6) Most people go through this drifting off and coming back process many times in a single meditation. With persistence we become adept at focusing our attention.

(7) The affirmation that you choose should be used throughout the day, not just during the meditation period. The readings encourage us to return to the spirit of the affirmation in each activity of our daily lives.

10. *Pray for others.*

The readings recommend that at the end of each meditation we take time to pray for others. Create two prayer lists that you can use for this part of the meditation session.

( ) A. The first list should consist of those situations or names of individuals for which you have been asked to pray. We can pray directly for them by sharing the energy that we have awakened in meditation. This sharing can be accomplished by our thoughts. The readings say that "Healing of every nature may be disseminated on the wings of thought."

( ) B. The second list consists of those individuals or situations for which we have concern but for which

we have not been asked to pray. The readings suggest that we say a prayer for protection in each of these cases.
[See the diagram on the next page, which depicts the steps you have completed.]

"If I had to give a person one suggestion as to how to alter or raise his consciousness, it would be to practice prayer and meditation. I don't know of *anything* that would mean more. I am the custodian of a little part of the Creative Energy. And I have to manage this; I have to work with it every day. In meditation and prayer I am able to allow this energy to move back towards a union with the Creative Energies of the universe. I think this is the grace and love of God. It is *constantly* available to me; however, I move to touch it only as I move my own consciousness back to a level that can relate to it. This is what I mean by meditation, prayer, and the quietness of attunement. There is nothing in the universe, that I've ever tried, that is more effective."   Hugh Lynn Cayce

REFERENCES

The Bhagavad-Gita. Translated by Swami Prabhavananda and Christopher Isherwood. New York: Mentor Books, 1954.
Carroll, Lewis. *Alice in Wonderland.* New York: Potter, 1973.
Govinda, Lama Anagarika. *Foundations of Tibetan Mysticism.* New York: Samuel Weiser, 1969.
Heywood, Rosalind. *ESP: A Personal Memoir.* New York: Dutton, 1964.
Jung, C.G. *Modern Man in Search of a Soul.* New York: Harcourt, Brace and World, 1933.
Jung, C.G. "The Archetypes and the Collective Unconscious." *The Collected Works of C.G. Jung,* vol. 9. Princeton: Princeton University Press, 1959.
Jung, C.G. "Psychology and Religion: West and East." *The Collected Works of C.G. Jung,* vol. 11. Princeton: Princeton University Press, 1959.
Kazantzakis, Nikos. *Saint Francis.* New York: Simon and Schuster, 1962.
Savary, Louis M. *Passages: A Guide for Pilgrims of the Mind.* New York: Harper and Row, 1972.
The Secret of the Golden Flower. Translated by Richard Wilhelm. Commentary by C.G. Jung. New York: Harcourt, Brace and World, 1962.
Underhill, Evelyn. *Mysticism: A Study in the Nature and Development of Man's Spiritual Consciousness.* New York: E.P. Dutton and Company, 1910.
The Upanishads. Selected and translated by Swami Prabhavananda and Frederick Manchester. New York: Mentor Books, 1952.

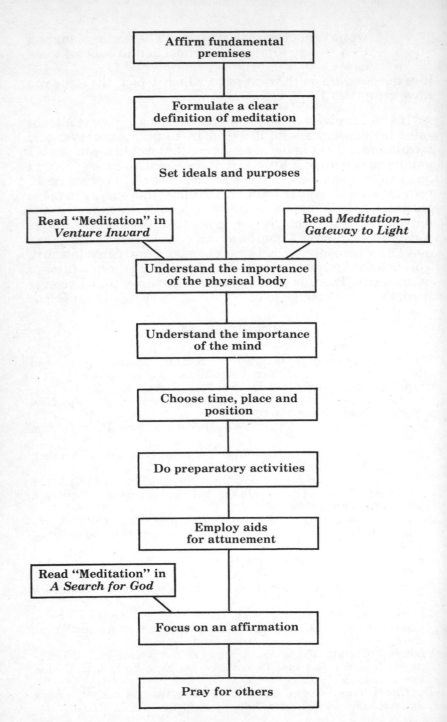

Affirm fundamental
premises

Formulate a clear
definition of meditation

Set ideals and purposes

Read "Meditation" in
Venture Inward

Read *Meditation—
Gateway to Light*

Understand the importance
of the physical body

Understand the importance
of the mind

Choose time, place and
position

Do preparatory activities

Employ aids
for attunement

Read "Meditation" in
A Search for God

Focus on an affirmation

Pray for others

What Is A.R.E.?

The Association for Research and Enlightenment, Inc. (A.R.E.®), is the international headquarters for the work of Edgar Cayce (1877-1945), who is considered the best-documented psychic of the twentieth century. Founded in 1931, the A.R.E. consists of a community of people from all walks of life and spiritual traditions, who have found meaningful and life-transformative insights from the readings of Edgar Cayce.

Although A.R.E. headquarters is located in Virginia Beach, Virginia—where visitors are always welcome—the A.R.E. community is a global network of individuals who offer conferences, educational activities, and fellowship around the world. People of every age are invited to participate in programs that focus on such topics as holistic health, dreams, reincarnation, ESP, the power of the mind, meditation, and personal spirituality.

In addition to study groups and various activities, the A.R.E. offers membership benefits and services, a bimonthly magazine, a newsletter, extracts from the Cayce readings, conferences, international tours, a massage school curriculum, an impressive volunteer network, a retreat-type camp for children and adults, and A.R.E. contacts around the world. A.R.E. also maintains an affiliation with Atlantic University, which offers a master's degree program in Transpersonal Studies.

For additional information about A.R.E. activities hosted near you, please contact:

A.R.E.
67th St. and Atlantic Ave.
P.O. Box 595
Virginia Beach, VA 23451-0595
(804) 428-3588